FLIP-O-MATIC

Ages 9-12

INSTANT SCIENCE

• Mark Shulman •

KAPLAN

Editorial Director: Jennifer Farthing
Editor: Megan Gilbert
Production Editor: David Shaw
Production Artist: Joe Budenholzer
Cover Designer: Carly Schnur
Illustrator: Amy Vangsgard

Published by Kaplan Publishing, a division of Kaplan, Inc.
888 Seventh Ave.
New York, NY 10106

Printed in the United States of America

July 2006
10 9 8 7 6 5 4 3 2 1

ISBN-13: 978-1-4195-4181-0
ISBN-10: 1-4195-4181-1

Kaplan Publishing books are available at special quantity discounts to use for sales promotions, employee premiums, or educational purposes. Please call our Special Sales Department to order or for more information at 800-621-9621, ext. 4444, e-mail kaplanpubsales@kaplan.com, or write to Kaplan Publishing, 30 South Wacker Drive, Suite 2500, Chicago, IL 60606-7481.

Your *Flip-O-Matic* Owner's Manual

Congratulations! You're the proud owner (or reader) of the very finest *Flip-O-Matic* Instant Science book you've ever seen. We know you're itching to open it up and take it for a spin...but first, please read this totally complicated introduction. We're sure you have a lot of questions about the book before you read all the questions in the book. Here are some questions we hope you'll ask.

WILL this book answer all my questions?

That depends on what all your questions are. But it will answer all our questions—250 of them, if you're counting. And if our questions happen to be the same as your questions, then the answer is a resounding YES!

WHY does this book have two covers?

All books have two covers. But the *Flip-O-Matic* has two covers that are front covers. This is twice as many front covers as almost any other book may have. It's like having two books in one! Our revolutionary *Flip-O-Matic* format allows us to save paper, and we pass those savings on to you.

ARE there more of these questions on the next page?

Yes!

WHO is Mark Shulman, and WHAT makes him an authority on this topic?

Mark Shulman is the author of dozens (12s) of books for people just like you. His books have titles like *The Brainiac Box: 600 Facts Every Smart Person Should Know* AND *Attack of the Killer Video Book* AND *Mom and Dad Are Palindromes* AND *Secret Hiding Places (for Clever Kids)*. He took science in middle school and can still pass it today!

WHAT do I do when I reach the end of the book?

When you get to the last question on this side of the book, just flip it over. That's why we call it a *Flip-O-Matic*. The beauty of this book is that, in fact, there is no end. It goes on forever. Talk about bang for your buck!

HOW, exactly, do I use my new *Flip-O-Matic* book?

It's just like any other question-and-answer book. Except it has two front covers—and twice the fun!

Have a flipping good time! Learn lots!

chemistry

Q: WHAT in the chemical world is an *element*?

A: The *Hubble Space Telescope*. It's the reason we've been able to see a comet collide with Jupiter, observe gamma-ray bursts, and seek out new life and new civilizations. It's expected to *deorbit* (drop out of the sky) in the year 2010. Wish us luck!

A: An *element* is a substance in its pure form. You can't break it down into another compound that has different properties, and neither can anyone else. It's also true that an element consists of atoms of one element.

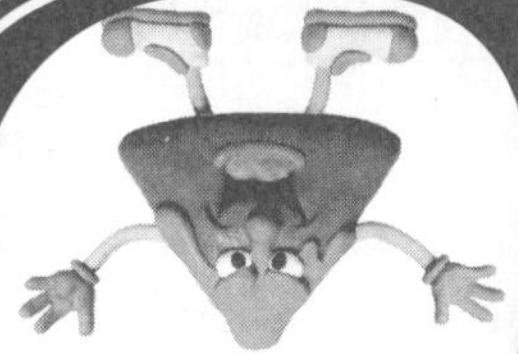

astronomy

Q: **WHAT** is the space telescope that revolutionized astronomy after its launch in 1990?

chemistry

Q: WHAT is an *atom*?

A: Every planet goes around the Sun in a different orbit, so its years are of different length. On Mercury, a year is 88 days long. On Jupiter, your birthday comes every 11.86 Earth years. And on Pluto, the calendars are 248 years long.

A: An *atom* (a word that comes from the Greek, meaning "can't be divided") is (1) really, really small; (2) found in all common matter; (3) the smallest part of an element to keep all its chemical properties; and (4) actually *can* be divided.

astronomy

Q: HOW long is a year on Mercury? On Jupiter? On Pluto?

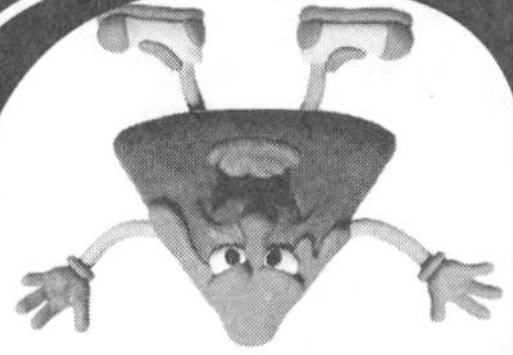

chemistry

Q: WHAT are the three subatomic part(icle)s that an atom can be divided into?

A: Jupiter, Saturn, Uranus, Neptune, Earth, Venus, Mars, Mercury, Pluto.

A: An atom can be divided into its electrons, protons, and neutrons.

astronomy

Q: WHAT are the nine planets, from largest to smallest?

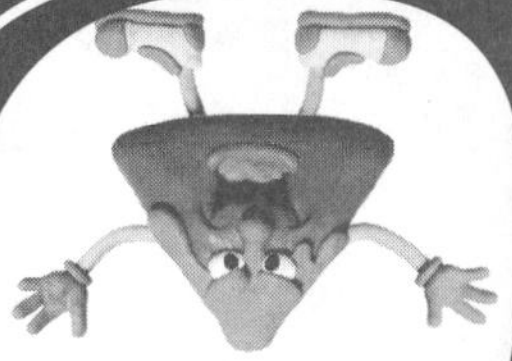

chemistry

Q: **WHAT** is a *molecule*?

A: Between Mars and Jupiter, there is a group of up to a million objects, smaller than planets, usually smaller than a mile across, and sometimes smaller than pebbles. The gravity of Jupiter and the Sun helps hold them in orbit. They are dangerous to spaceships and are good protection against an attack from Saturn.

A: When two atoms (or more) are joined together (chemically), a *molecule* is formed. O_2 (oxygen) is a molecule but it isn't a compound. But what is a compound, you ask? So do we. Flip to the next page...

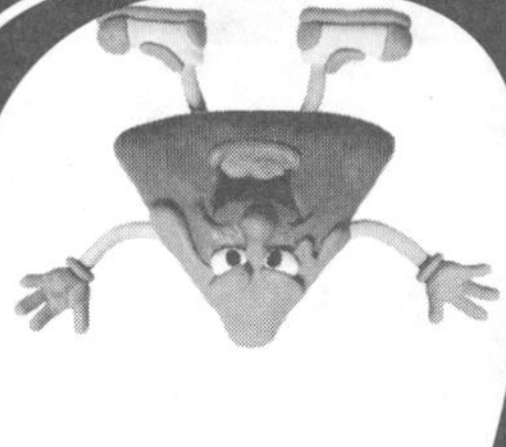

Q: WHICH two planets have the asteroid belt between them?

astronomy

chemistry

Q: WHAT is a *compound?*

A: A *meteoroid* is a rather small space chunk (under 170 feet in diameter) entering a planet's atmosphere. Whether it's mineral or ice, as it heats up during entry it gets a bright tail of glowing gas that's called a *meteor*. (If you wish upon it, it's called a *shooting star*.) Any fragment that actually reaches the ground is called a *meteorite*.

A: A *compound* is a molecule whose atoms contain at least two different elements. Dihydrogen oxide (H_2O) is a compound of hydrogen and oxygen, and carbon dioxide (CO_2) is a compound of carbon and oxygen. Remember, all molecules are compounds, but all compounds are not molecules.

astronomy

Q: **WHAT** is the difference between a meteoroid, a meteor, and a meteorite?

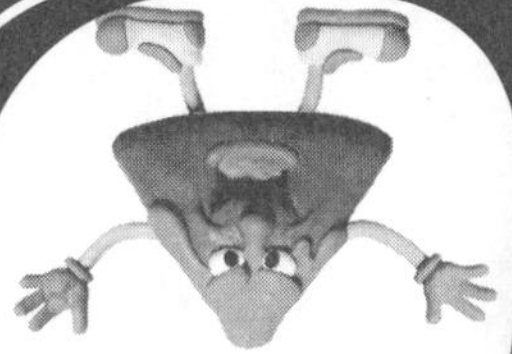

chemistry

Q: WHICH subatomic particles have a positive charge, and which have a negative charge?

A: Every rock and near-rock in space is reflecting the light of the Sun or another star. Nothing but a star generates its own light.

A: Protons have a positive charge, and electrons have a negative charge. Neutrons are neutral and have no charge at all.

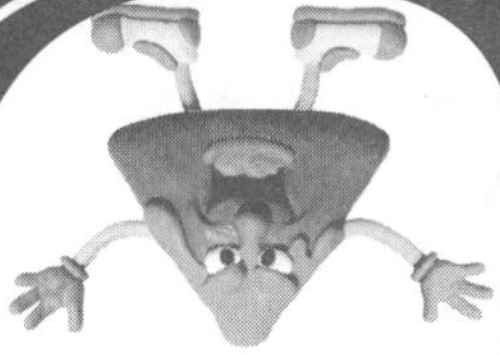

astronomy

Q: WHAT makes the Moon and the planets visible in the inky darkness of space?

chemistry

Q: WHAT are the three states of matter? (Think water.)

A: Earth is about 50 million miles from Mars. Using current rocket technology, it would take about four months to get there. Using a car, it would take even longer.

A: Solid, liquid, and gas.

astronomy

Q: **HOW** far is Earth from Mars?

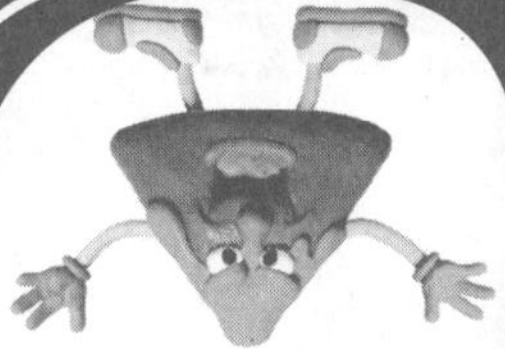

chemistry

Q: HOW does matter change between solid, liquid, and gas?

A: About 28 million miles away. Venus and Earth are always moving, like sumo wrestlers, so it's hard to be exact.

A: The scientific answer: The molecular motion changes, usually due to heat. The unscientific answer: boiling and freezing.

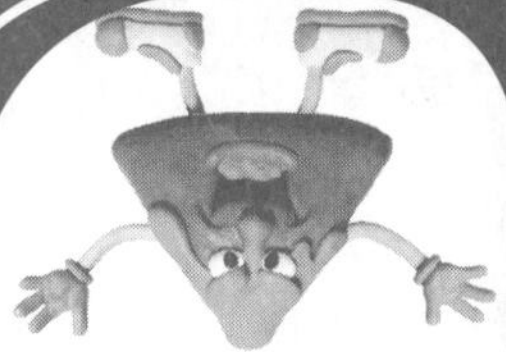

Q: HOW far is Venus from Earth?

astronomy

chemistry

Q: WHAT is known as *the fourth state of matter?*

A: It takes just over eight minutes for sunlight to travel 93 million miles. So, if the Sun suddenly stops working, we'll have about 480 extra seconds to work on our tans.

A: It isn't gas, liquid, or solid. It's *plasma!* It conducts electricity and, recently, TV shows.

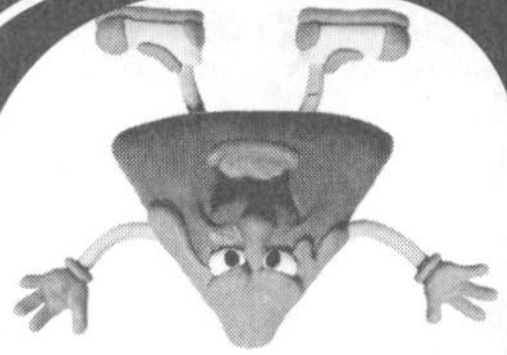

astronomy

Q: **HOW** old is sunlight by the time it reaches Earth?

chemistry

Q: WHEN atoms and molecules move most freely, what state is the matter in?

A: About 93 million miles, more or less.

A: Gas. When atoms and molecules are loosely connected, they create liquids. And when they are tightly connected, and can't move, the results are totally solid.

astronomy

Q: HOW far is the Sun from the Earth?

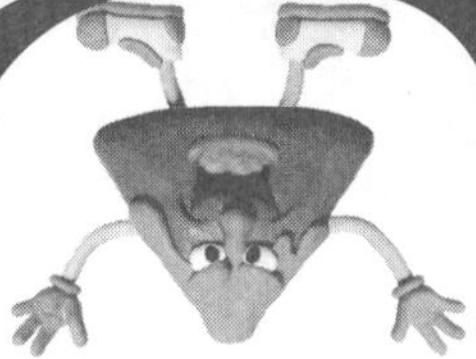

chemistry

Q: **WHAT** is the *periodic table of elements?*

A: The speed of light is about *186,000 miles per second.* The Moon is about 250,000 miles away. Pretty fast.

A: The *periodic table of elements* is the most valuable tool in chemistry—it describes the different properties of each chemical element. Each element appears in numerical order, based on how many electrons it has. For example, hydrogen (#1) has one electron. Helium (#2) has two electrons, and so on.

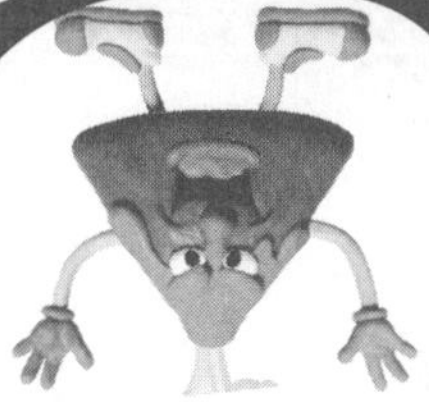

Q: HOW fast is the speed of light (in seconds)?

astronomy

chemistry

Q: HOW many elements have been discovered (so far)?

A: The Milky Way is about 90 thousand light years in diameter. To get a better idea of its size: If the Milky Way were 100 miles in diameter, our solar system would be about a tenth of an inch wide.

A: There are currently 103 elements, and all of them are featured on the periodic table. Some elements, like hydrogen, oxygen, and carbon, are found in every living organism. Others, like lawrencium (under the table at #103), have a half-life of a few seconds and then decay beyond recognition, which is what usually happens under the table.

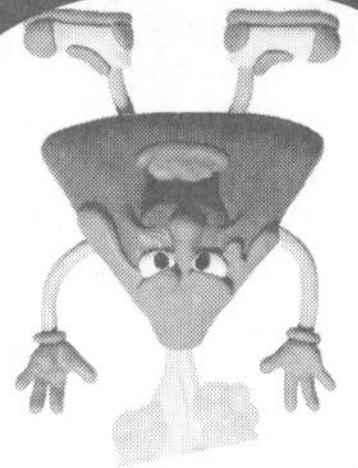

Q: HOW wide is the Milky Way, in light years?

astronomy

chemistry

Q: WHAT super man's name is found on the periodic table of the elements?

A: A light year measures distance, not time. It's used to measure gigantic distances. It's the amount of distance that light travels in a year: six trillion (6,000,000,000,000) miles.

A: ClArK is his name. Chlorine, argon, and potassium (atomic numbers 17, 18, 19) are his secret ingredients. You may wonder why potassium is represented with a K, and so do we.

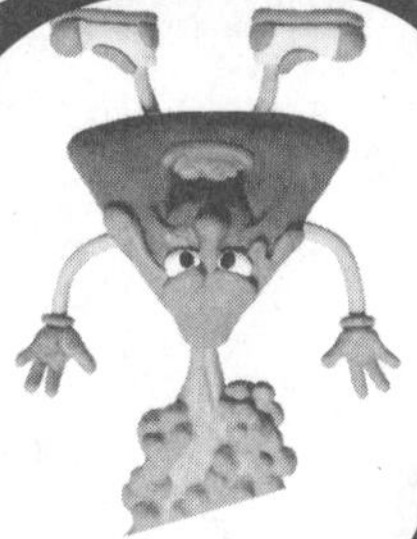

astronomy

Q: WHAT does a light year measure?

chemistry

Q: WHAT changes during a chemical reaction?

A: There are about 100 billion stars in our galaxy. And it's not nearly the biggest one.

A: During a chemical reaction the atoms in matter are rearranged into new, different, and occasionally life-threatening combinations of molecules.

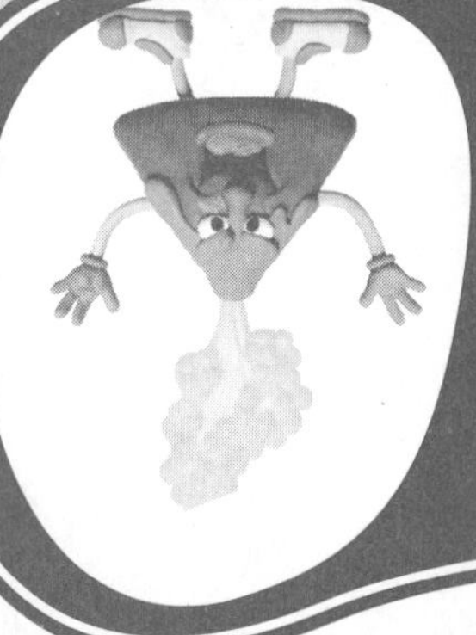

astronomy

Q: HOW many stars are in the Milky Way galaxy: about 100, about 100 thousand, about 100 million, or about 100 billion?

chemistry

Q: WHICH two ways can matter change form without a chemical reaction?

A: A *galaxy* is a massive star cluster. Some have a few million stars, others have over a trillion stars clinging together. All these stars share a common center of gravity. Our galaxy is called the Milky Way, and there are billions more next door.

A: Matter can freeze and matter can boil, and all without a chemical reaction.

astronomy

Q: WHAT is a galaxy?

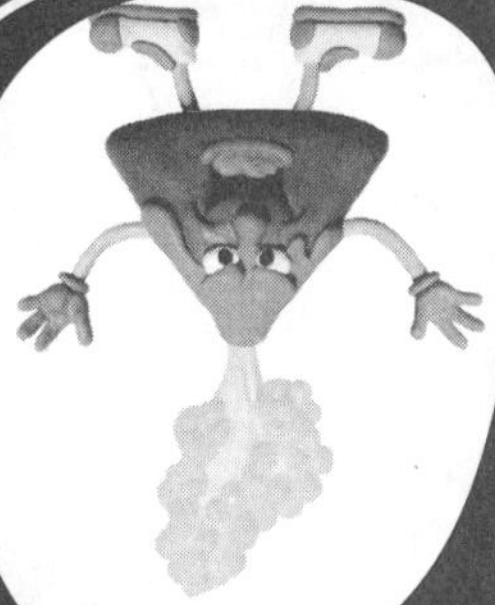

chemistry

Q: **WHAT** happens to heat during *most* chemical reactions?

A: Because the Earth is caught in the Sun's gravitational attraction. It's an attraction that has lasted for more than 4 billion years.

A: Heat is either absorbed or released. And, therefore, your result is either something that got colder (absorbed heat) or hotter (released heat).

astronomy

Q: WHY does the Earth revolve around the Sun?

chemistry

Q: WHAT happens to the number of atoms in matter during a chemical reaction?

A: A *planetary system* is any group of planets (and their moons) orbiting a star, or stars—plus whatever asteroids, meteoroids, and comets are caught in the stellar gravity. But there's only one *solar system*, and that's ours—the planetary system that orbits the sun named *Sol*.

A: Trick question: Nothing happens. The number of atoms (the matter's *mass*) stays the same even after a chemical reaction.

astronomy

Q: WHAT is the difference between the terms *solar system* and *planetary system*?

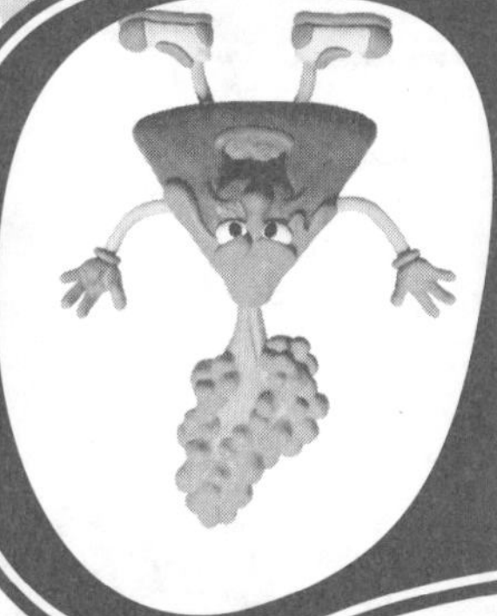

chemistry

Q: **WHAT** does pH measure?

A: Different amounts of the "light" side of the Moon are visible at different times of the month. The Moon *seems* like a circle or a crescent at different times of the month because the Moon, Earth, and Sun are always changing positions.

A: pH measures the acidity (acid) or alkalinity (base) of water or a solution. Acidity is the presence of acid in the solution. Base is the lack of acid but the presence of alkaline. Neutral is neutral.

astronomy

Q: WHY does the Moon seem to change shape?

chemistry

Q: WHICH color will litmus paper change to when dipped in an acid solution?

A: The new moon occurs when the Earth, the Sun, and the Moon are in a straight line. The Earth is in the middle, and it's casting a shadow on the Moon.

A: When litmus paper is dipped in an acid solution, litmus paper turns red. FYI, when it's dipped in a base solution, it turns blue.

astronomy

Q: WHY can't we see a new moon?

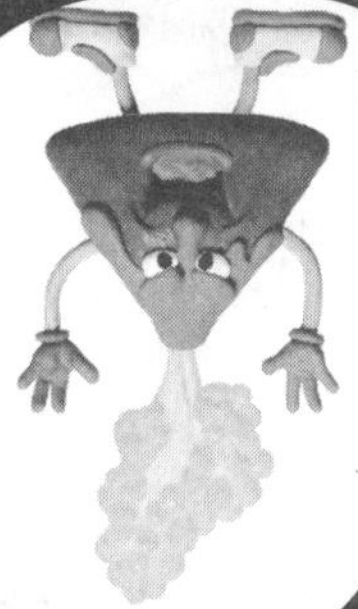

earth science

Q: **WHO** studies rocks and the planet?

A: Because the Moon doesn't revolve as it orbits Earth. The so-called "light side" always faces us, and the so-called "dark side" is always turned away. Actually, neither side is always light or dark: Each has days, just like we do.

A: Lots of people do. But *geologists* get paid for it, usually.

astronomy

Q: WHY is there a "dark side of the Moon"?

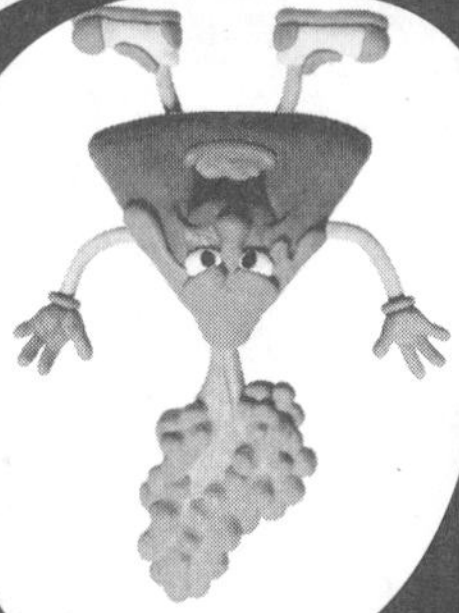

earth science

Q: WHAT three layers make up the Earth?

A: About 1.3 million Earths would fit inside. Imagine filling a basketball (Sun) with sesame seeds (Earths).

A: The *core*, the *mantle*, and the *crust* (or *lithosphere*). You live on the upper crust.

astronomy

Q: **HOW** many Earths would fit inside the Sun if it were hollow?

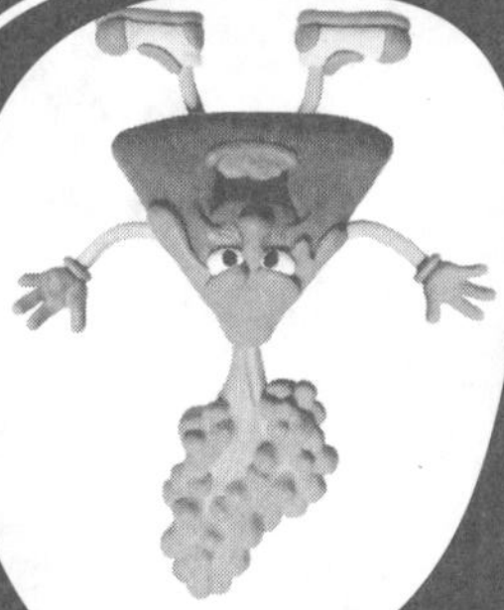

earth science

Q: WHAT is the Earth's crust? **WHAT** is it made of?

A: Average. The Sun is about 865,000 miles in diameter. Other stars are as much as 1,500 times larger.

A: The crust (also called the *lithosphere*) is the outermost surface of the Earth. The top layer is soil (or *dirt*), and different rock layers come next, before reaching the mantle about 18 miles under your house.

astronomy

Q: **HOW** does the Sun rank in size compared to other stars: above average, below average, or average?

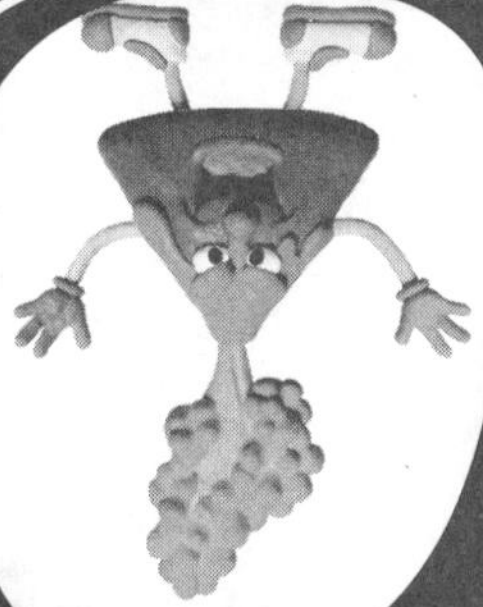

earth science

Q: **WHERE** on Earth is the planet's *mantle*?

A: The *Sun* is a ball of burning gas. Most of it (*70* percent) is hydrogen, and 28 percent is helium.

A: The *crust* is the Earth's *outermost* layer. The 1,800 miles beneath it is called the *mantle*, reaching all the way to the Earth's inner core. Imagine a popular, grape-sized, colorful, candy-coated, brand name chocolate treat with a peanut in the center. The candy coating is the crust. The chocolate is the mantle. The peanut is the core. *Yum!*

astronomy

Q: WHAT is the *Sun* made of?

earth science

Q: WHEN it comes to soil, what is its parent material?

A: If you don't count man-made satellites, falling space stations, and random asteroids, the answer is the *Moon*.

A: *Parent material* is what's in the bedrock below the soil. Minerals from the bedrock influence the soil, just like a sloppy mess influences the sponge you clean it with.

astronomy

Q: WHAT is the closest astronomical object to the planet Earth?

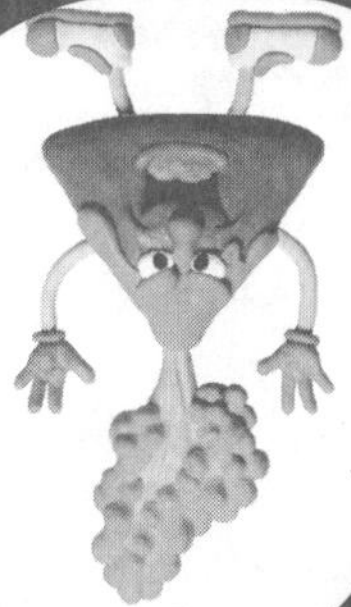

earth science

Q: WHICH three chemicals are almost always found in the parent material of soil?

A: The universe is only 10–20 billion years old. And you thought your parents were old.

astronomy

Q: HOW many years old is the universe: 10–20 billion, 20–30 billion, or 30–40 billion years?

A: Alphabetically speaking, *calcium*, *nitrogen*, and *sulfur*.

earth science

Q: WHAT is *plate tectonics?*

A: Our solar system is 4.6 billion years old. Compared with the universe, that's still kind of young.

A: *Plate tectonics* describes the motion of enormous plates—or sections—of the Earth's crust and upper mantle. Imagine a hairpiece sliding very slowly across a bald man's head. Now imagine several moving at the same time. Awful thought, isn't it?

astronomy

Q: HOW many years old is our solar system: 1.6 billion, 4.6 billion, or 9.6 billion years?

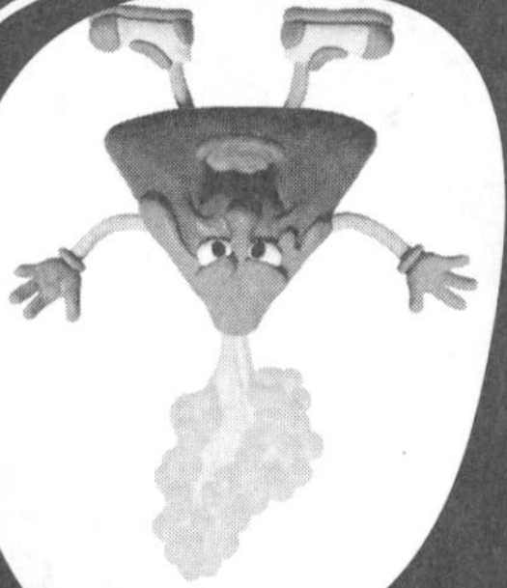

Q: **HOW** quickly do the Earth's plates move?

A: The planet (not the dog) is mostly ice, with some rock mixed in. It's two-thirds the size of Earth's moon and 4.3 billion miles away. You'd hate it there. You'd only get a birthday once every 249 years.

A: When they're not causing massive geophysical mayhem, the Earth's massive plates generally move a few inches a year. When they go faster than that, it makes headlines.

astronomy

Q: **WHAT** is Pluto made of?

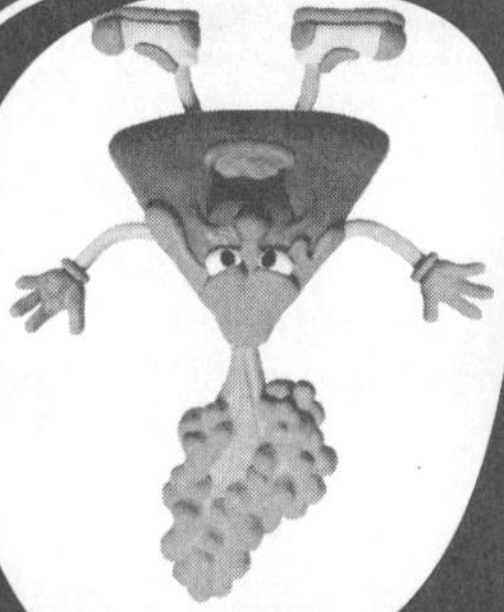

earth science

Q: WHY do the Earth's plates shift?

A: One, two, three, and four: *Mercury*, *Venus*, *Mars*, and especially *Earth* are made of earth. (That's what *terrestrial* means, you Earthling.)

A: The Earth's mantle is a restless place. It's extremely hot, but not consistent. As it gets (relatively) cooler and then heats back up (a process called *convection*) the mantle's molten contents expand and contract in very slow motion, causing plates to shift.

astronomy

Q: WHICH planets in our solar system are *terrestrial*, and what in the world does that mean?

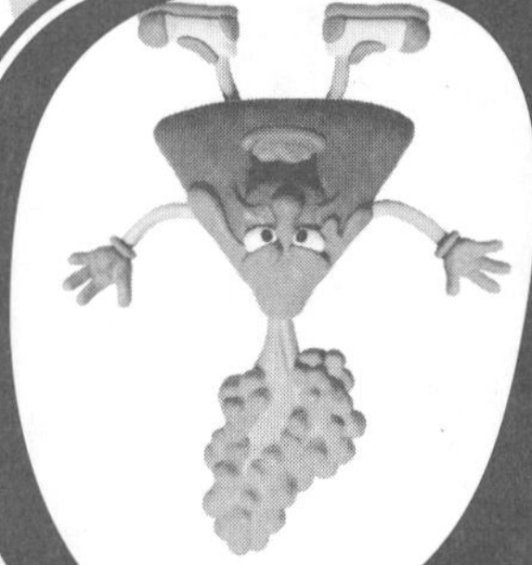

earth science

Q: **WHEN** the Earth's plates shift, what happens?

A: Five, six, seven, and eight: *Jupiter*, *Saturn*, *Uranus*, and *Neptune* are each composed mainly of gases. In fact, if *Saturn* could be lowered onto water, it would actually float. These four "gas giants" make up 99 percent of the mass orbiting our *Sun*.

A: Earthquakes happen. Tsunamis happen, as a result of underwater earthquakes. Mountains happen as landforms are redefined. And volcanoes happen as bubbling hot magma flows through new openings in the Earth's surface.

astronomy

Q: WHICH of the nine original planets in our solar system are gas planets?

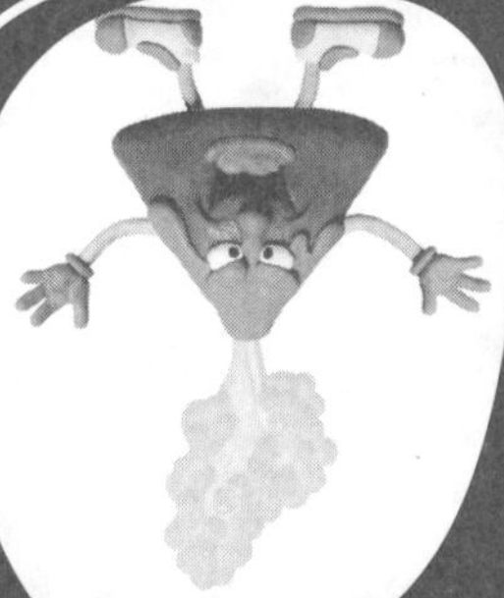

Q: WHAT do earthquakes and fingernail biting have in common?

A: Flux! In a state of flux, everything is constantly changing—whether it's growing, decaying, moving, or otherwise evolving. With stasis, nothing changes.

A: *Stress!* In the case of earthquakes, stress exists at the Earth's faults, where the tectonic plates are either colliding or separating. In the case of fingernails, relax! Problems have a way of working themselves out.

astronomy

Q: **WHICH** word best describes the state of everything in the Earth, the solar system, and the universe: *stasis* or *flux?*

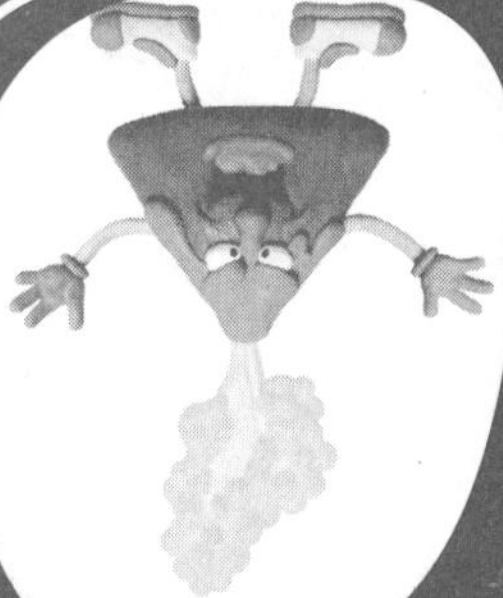

Q: WHAT are *stalagmites* and *stalactites*?

A: It's as easy as 1 and 2. Type 1 is mainly for water and soda bottles. Type 2 is for milk bottles, detergent bottles, and many plastic bags. Some Type 4 bags (garment bags and shrink wrap) can be recycled. Rarely can the rest. But the worst offender is Type 7, mixed or layered plastic, which has no redeeming (or redeemable) features and must be landfilled.

A: These icicle-shaped formations are usually found in caves. They're made from a mix of dripping water, calcium, and other minerals. *Stalactites* hang from the ceiling and drip down, forming *stalagmites* that rise up from the ground. (Remember, *c* is for *ceiling* and *g* is for *ground*.)

ecology

Q: **WHICH** of the numbers—from 1 to 7—stamped on a plastic container represent plastic that's recyclable?

earth science

Q: WHAT is *sedimentary rock?*

A: Everything plastic, including a higher percentage of your clothing than you'd care to know, is made from *petrochemicals*. The *chemicals* part is no surprise. The *petro* part is oil. That's right. You're wearing oil. As oil prices go up (and supplies go down), so too will the prices you pay for your cola bottle, your garden hose, your computer keyboard, your eyeglass frames, and those stylish, former plastic bottles that are now your fleece jacket. Paper or plastic?

A: *Sedimentary rock* (meaning *settled* rock) is formed from sand, dust, seashells, and sea creatures that settled at the ocean's bottom, many millions of years ago. Over time, the layers hardened into rock. Limestone is a sedimentary rock popular with fossil hunters.

ecology

Q: **WHAT** is plastic made from?

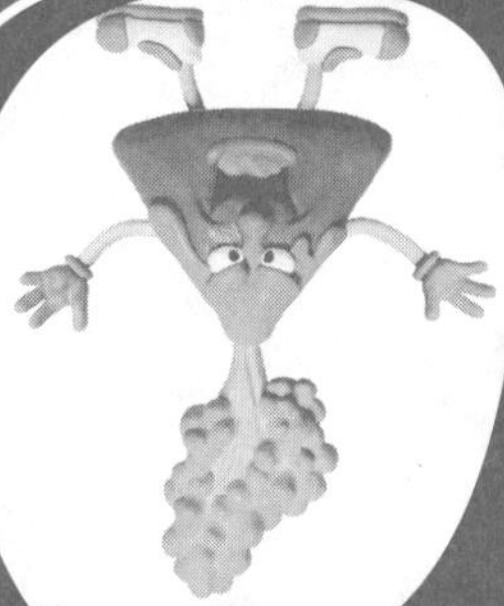

Q: **WHAT** is *metamorphic* rock?

A: The Sun (solar panels), wind (windmills), water (hydroelectric generators), geysers and hot springs (geothermal exchange pumps), and certain crops (biofuel converters) are renewable. It actually is easy being green, and some day, it'll be easier to power your life more naturally.

A: *Metamorphic* rock (meaning *changed* rock) lies beneath sedimentary rock. For example, heat and pressure inside the Earth cause limestone to morph into marble over a very long time. Shale also turns into slate this way.

ecology

Q: WHICH of Earth's energy sources are renewable?

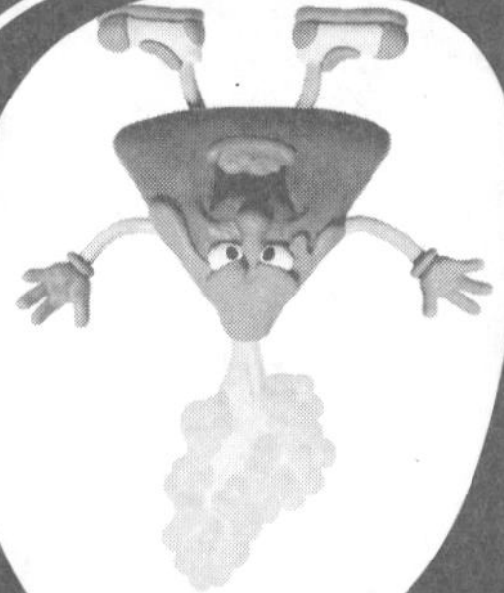

earth science

Q: WHAT is *igneous* rock?

A: Like the most popular library books, some sources of energy can't be renewed. Coal, for instance. Once you use it, it's burnt up. Gone. Up in smoke. Nothing left behind. Same goes for oil and gas. And if you *really* want to name an energy source you'd never want to renew, that's nuclear energy. Its endless barrels of toxic byproduct are a total waste.

A: *Igneous* rock (meaning *fired* rock) is melted rock, or *magma*, that squeezes through cracks in the Earth's crust. When it cools and hardens, it's one tough rock. Take it for granite.

ecology

Q: WHICH of Earth's energy sources are non-renewable?

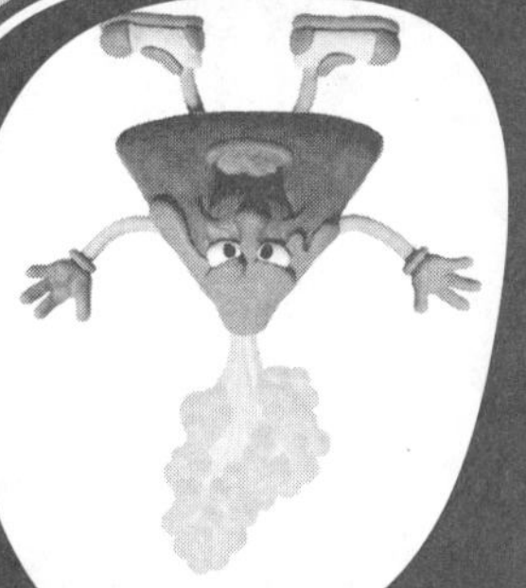

earth science

Q: **WHAT** would you find between the Earth's crust and its mantle?

A: In alphabetical order: coal, gas, hydroelectric, nuclear, oil, solar, and wind.

A: *Magma* (meaning *melted* rock) is the checkpoint between the Earth's top two layers. It's hot. It's bubbly. And it's the inspiration for volcanoes all over the world.

ecology

Q: **WHAT** are the seven leading (or most common) energy sources on Earth?

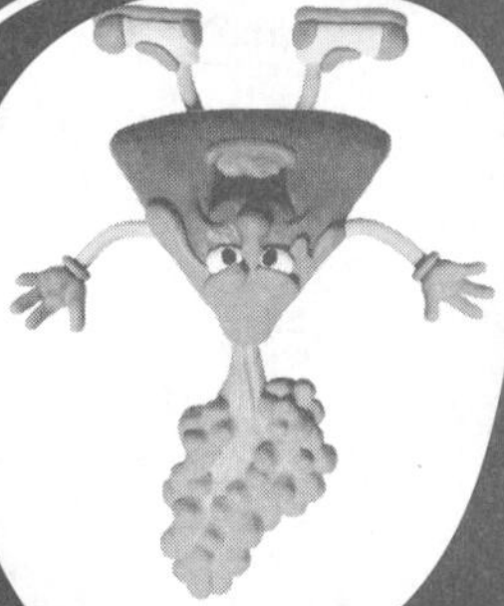

earth science

Q: WHAT is the Earth's mantle made of?

A: A *hypothesis* is a theory about the natural world that tries to explain certain facts or observations.

A: Solid rock. Hot rock. 1,000°–3,000° rock. And it rocks from about 18 miles underfoot to about 1,800 miles.

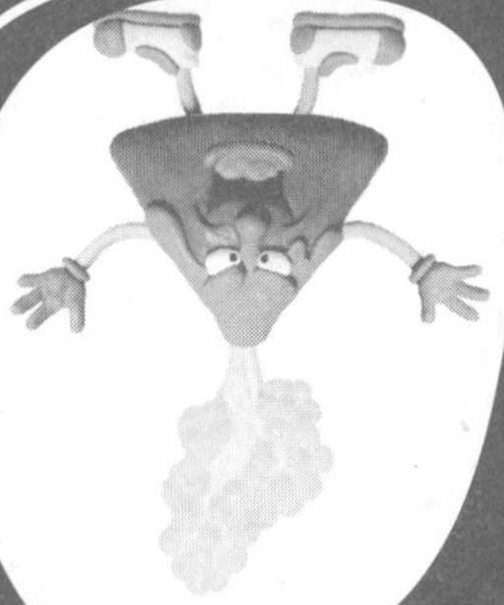

Q: WHAT is a *hypothesis?*

ecology

earth science

Q: WHAT is the Earth's core made of?

A: A *scale map* shows a printed area that's a percentage of the actual area it represents. If a ten-inch map reflects a ten-mile area, the scale is one inch equals one mile. If it's a map of the solar system, one inch could be 100 million miles.

A: Heavy metal. Around 80 percent is iron—the rest is estimated to be liquid iron, nickel, and other metals. The inner core may even be a single iron crystal. You can proudly say you live on the densest planet in the solar system.

ecology

Q: WHAT is a scale map?

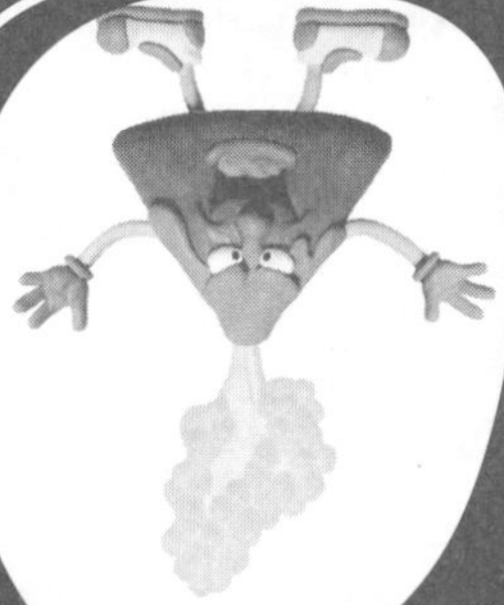

earth science

Q: HOW big is the Earth's core?

A: A topographic map shows the natural and man-made features of a place, including landscape and elevations. A geologic map shows the geology of an area: the sedimentary, igneous and volcanic formations, and geologic structures (like folds and faults). Neither is a *political map*, which tells you what city or country you're in and, like politics, is always subject to change.

A: The core is divided into two parts: the inner core and the outer core. The radius of the outer core is about 2,200 miles. The radius of the central inner core is about 800 miles.

geology

Q: **WHAT** is the difference between a topographic map and a geologic map?

earth science

Q: HOW long is the radius of the Earth?

A: Pen, pencil, paper, chalkboard, computer, calculator, microscope, magnifying glass, binoculars, telescope, camera, scale, stethoscope, and on and on.

A: All in all, the Earth's radius is about 4,000 miles from surface to core. If you're going, you won't need a sweater. It'll be warm when you get there.

ecology

Q: WHAT are some of the many tools used by scientists to collect data?

earth science

Q: **WHAT** on Earth is the *geosphere*?

A: When a species, a queen, or a president gets replaced by something else, it's called succession.

A: The *geosphere* includes every system on Earth: the atmosphere, the biosphere, the hydrosphere, and the lithosphere.

ecology

Q: WHAT is it called when some species eventually get replaced by others in an ecosystem?

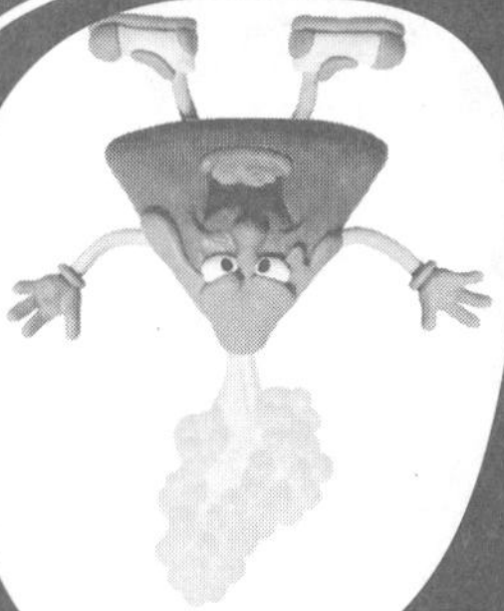

earth science

Q: **WHAT** role have asteroids played in shaping the Earth and the Moon?

A: If you combine the total mass of every organism in a particular ecosystem, you get the biomass. (bio + mass = get it?)

A: On Earth, asteroid collisions are thought to have caused *radical climate shifts*, such as the ice ages, which wiped out dinosaurs and other species. It's easier to see what asteroids did for the Moon's beauty—guess what caused those lovely craters?

ecology

Q: **WHAT** is *biomass?*

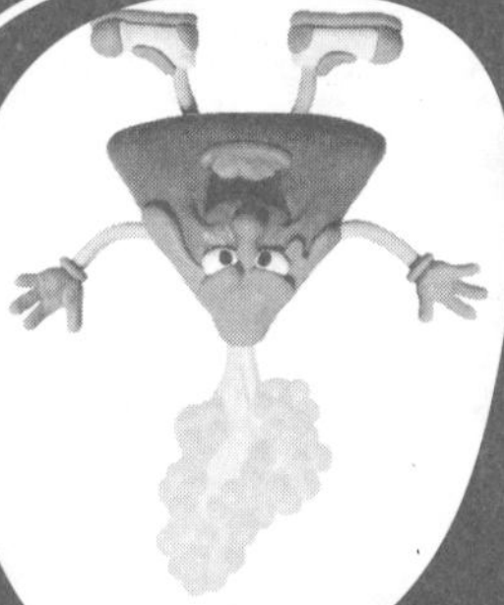

Q: WHAT is a *rock cycle*, and did cave dwellers ride them?

A: Energy arrives with the bright light of the sun. Producers convert sunlight into chemical energy during photosynthesis.

A: A *rock cycle* is a series of changes that rocks can go through. Under different conditions, igneous, sedimentary, or metamorphic rock can change into igneous, sedimentary, or metamorphic rock. If cave dwellers did ride them, it was downhill all the way.

Q: HOW does energy first enter an ecosphere?

ecology

earth science

Q: WHICH word describes the speed of the Earth's usual geologic processes (in the cases that do not involve asteroid collisions)?

A: Producers convert sunlight into chemical energy during photosynthesis. A vegetarian consumes the plant, and a carnivore consumes the vegetarian. Everybody ultimately dies and decomposes, making rich soil. Producers grow. And so on.

A: *Slow.* Or perhaps, *glacial.* Generally, real change takes place over very long periods of time. Like epochs or eras. We're talking *millions* of years.

ecology

Q: **HOW** is matter transferred between organisms in a food web?

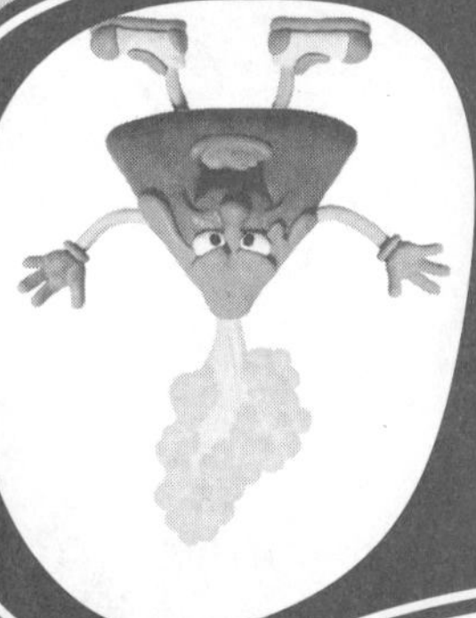

earth science

Q: WHAT exactly do volcanoes change on Earth?

A:

1. *Producers* are organisms, like green plants, that others find tasty.
2. *Consumers* get nutrients from other organisms, and find them tasty.
3. *Decomposers* (or *saprobes*) convert dead things into substances that are definitely not tasty but help producers grow.

A: Those murderous, molten mountains change the very topographic surface of the Earth. When the bubbling, red-hot magma cools down, mountains are raised, islands are formed, seashores are altered, and mapmakers everywhere get back to work.

ecology

Q: WHAT three roles can organisms play as they exchange energy on the food chain?

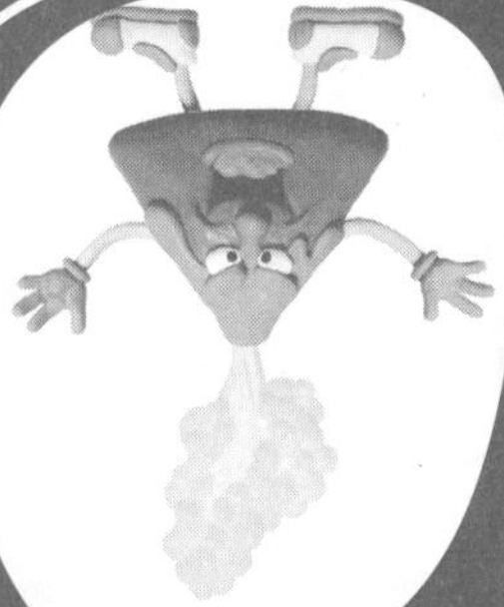

earth science

Q: WHAT comes out of a volcano when it erupts?

A: Roughly translated, *adaptation* means "changing whatever traits need changing, in order to help a species live longer." Adaptation improves an organism's odds of survival—and reproduction—in the world.

A: Mostly there's *magma* (molten rock) from inside the Earth's surface. Once it comes out, it's called *lava*. Volcanic ash and rocks and dust also emerge, as would skeletons and buried treasure if they happened to be near the source of the eruption at the time and didn't melt easily.

ecology

Q: WHAT is *adaptation?*

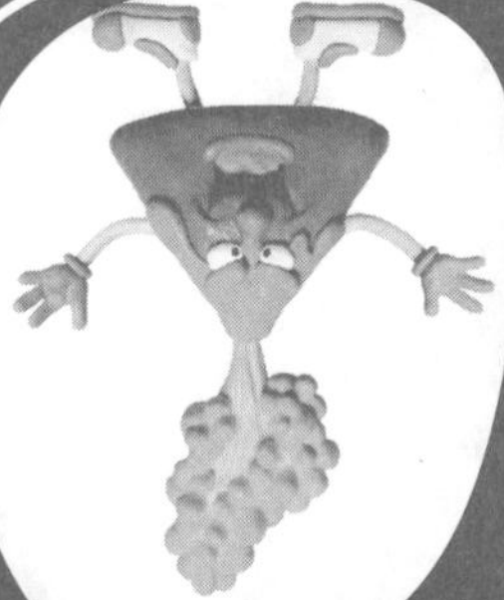

earth science

Q: WHAT are *fossils?*

A: Any ecologist will tell you that the official definition of sustainability is "meeting the needs of the present generation (natural resources, open space, protected species, etc.) without compromising the ability of future generations to meet their own." That ecologist will also tell you that this generation is barely leaving future generations enough to sustain themselves with.

A: *Fossils* are the remains of animals or plants, or eggs, or footprints...all turned into rocks or minerals.

ecology

Q: WHAT is *sustainability?*

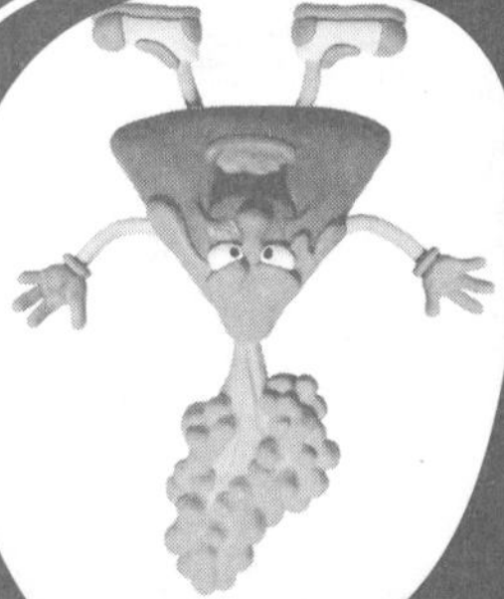

earth science

Q: **HOW** do innocent little animals and plants get turned into fossils?

A: What sounds like a shoe tread is actually a measure of the amount of land, water, and other natural resources needed by the human population of a specific area. The ecological footprint of a city block in Manhattan is far greater than of a farm in Kansas. Waste products are also measured.

A: Since living things tend to decompose after they've bitten the dust, becoming a fossil isn't easy. The corpse in question has to be covered with sediment relatively soon, or settle underwater, or become petrified. Natural decomposition is slowed or stopped. More sediment settles, hardens, and gradually becomes a rock cast of the original model. This can happen with footprints and other marks, too.

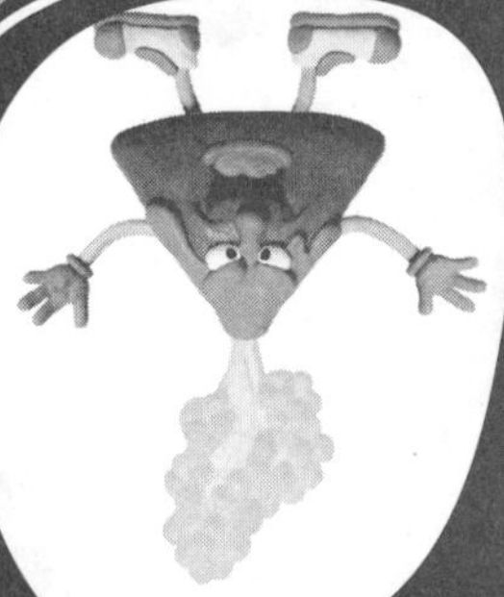

ecology

Q: WHAT is an ecological footprint?

earth science

Q: HOW old are the oldest fossils?

A: *Humans* are nature's most natural disrupters. Whether we over-fish the oceans, overbuild our neighborhoods, or over-pollute our air, human carelessness causes imbalance, and puts the *eeek!* into the world's ecosystems.

A: Would you believe 3.5 billion years old? The oldest known fossils are of *stromatolites*. They were trapped in once-gooey sheets of cyanobacteria, way back when. Some scientists believe that some simple life forms date back even further, to 3.8 billion years. That doesn't sound like a big jump, from 3.5 billion to 3.8, until you realize .3 billion adds another 300 million years to the equation.

ecology

Q: WHAT is the biggest threat to any ecosystem?

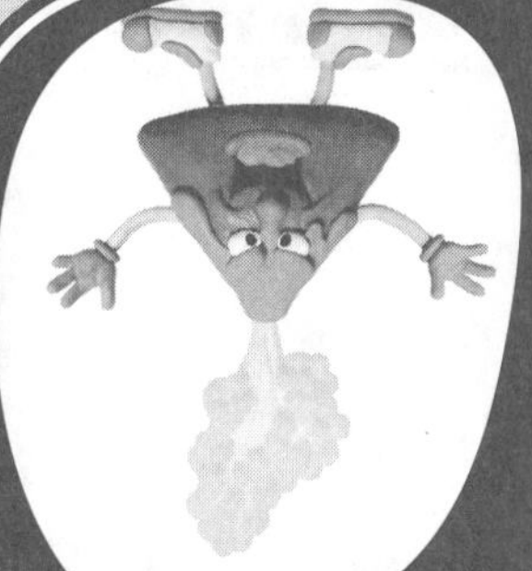

earth science

Q: WHY are fossils important, other than being cool to look at?

A: An ecosystem is an interconnected *group of living things*. Animals, plants, insects, and more create delicate biotic communities as big as an ocean or as small as a garden.

A: Fossils let us see changes in environmental conditions and life over millions or even billions of years. They can help scientists discover the date of the era or epoch when the fossil originally lived. And some of the medium-sized fossils make great doorstops.

ecology

Q: WHAT is an ecosystem?

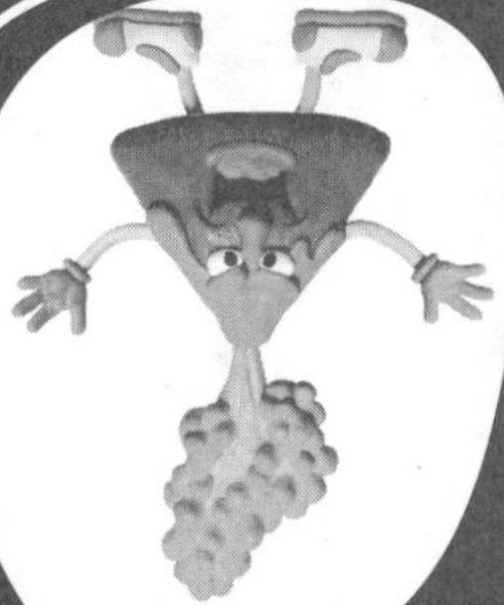

earth science

Q: **WHAT** do you call people who study fossils?

A: Ecologists study the many ways that living things interact with their environment—and how environments affect living things. You could also say that ecologists study the ecology, but isn't that obvious?

A: You probably call them *paleontologists*, unless they're your Aunt Betty and Uncle Gene. Then you call them Aunt Betty and Uncle Gene. You may be thinking that paleontologists only study dinosaurs. No, they study all the old fossils. But dinosaurs are the "big time" of paleontology.

ecology

Q: WHAT do ecologists study?

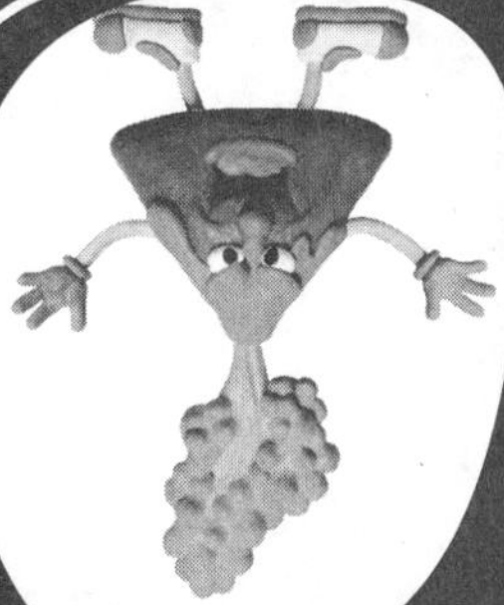

earth science

Q: WHAT system do scientists use in determining the age of a fossil or other geological specimen?

A: Hydrogen, nitrogen, oxygen, carbon, phosphorus, and sulfur.

A: They use radioactive dating. The best-known form of radioactive dating is carbon-14 dating.

biology

Q: **WHICH** elements are found in the molecules of every living organism?

earth science

Q: WHAT is *carbon-14 dating?*

A: Carbon. It can combine in many ways and is so very everywhere that finding the age of the carbon in any organism (carbon dating) is the scientific means of telling the object's age.

A: *Carbon-14* (radioactive) *dating* tells you when something died (but not how old it was). Basically, all living things are mostly made of carbon. Some of this carbon is C-14. When the organism dies, its C-14 starts disintegrating at a predictable rate. Scientists simply (?) measure how much C-14 is left, do some math, and then come up with an answer like "23 thousand years old." It's that easy.

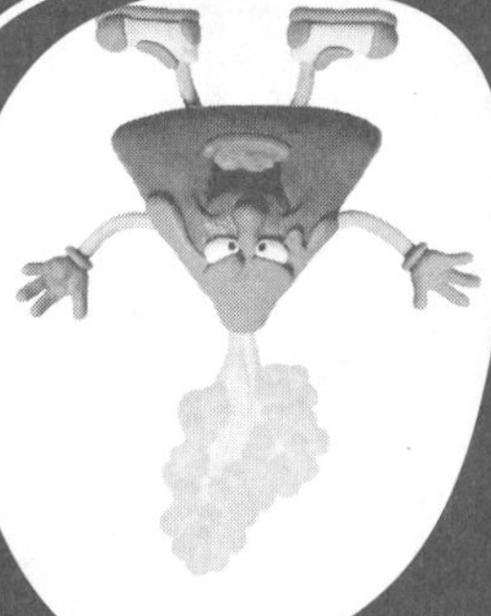

Q: **WHICH** common element is so common and so flexible, it has a main role in the chemistry of living organisms?

biology

earth science

Q: WHAT (besides radioactive dating) also gives important clues about the Earth's history?

A: The wrist and ankle joints work like hinges. The shoulder and hip are ball-and-socket joints, where the ball at the end of the upper arm or leg swivels around in the torso.

A: Geologic layers give plenty of evidence to geologists, paleontologists, and well-diggers. Each geologic period left its own unique debris, with ice ages in between leaving "lines" like the rings of a tree.

biology

Q: WHERE on your body can you find a hinge, and a ball-and-socket, just like on a machine?

earth science

Q: **HOW** long has life on Earth been on Earth?

A: The valves prevent blood from flowing back into the heart the wrong way.

A: Life on Earth began on Earth between 3.5 and 4 billion years ago, possibly on a Monday. The Earth itself is estimated to be 4.5 billion years old. The Sun is also estimated to be about 4.5 billion years old. This is not a coincidence.

biology

Q: WHAT is the job of the heart's valves?

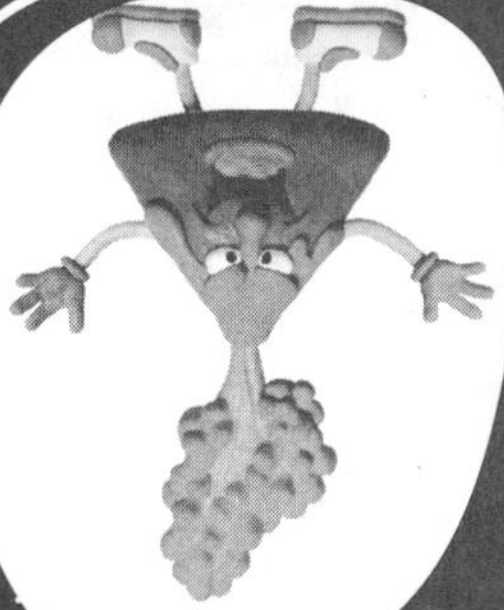

earth science

Q: WHAT is the main reason life has been so well distributed on every continent?

A: The pumping heart is doing it's job, generating blood pressure to circulate blood.

A: You can thank the ever-shifting continental and oceanic plates. The continents that broke away from the main mass (Eurasia) brought all sorts of life with them as they drifted away.

biology

Q: WHAT happens to an animal when its heart contracts?

earth science

Q: HOW has climate determined the way organisms are distributed throughout the planet?

A: In telescopes, microscopes, magnifying glasses, camera lenses, and the eye.

A: Organisms, like everyone else, like to go where there's food, habitat, and a chance for survival. And anyone, even an organism, is going to thrive where the climate is hospitable. A look at the Earth's climate zones reveals the greatest abundance, and diversity of organisms in the most hospitable (read: pleasant) climates.

biology

Q: **WHERE** can you find simple lenses?

earth science

Q: WHAT is an *ice age?*

A: White light is a mixture of many colors, which are each a different wavelength. On the flip side, black is not a color but the total absence of color.

A: An *ice age* is a long period of below-freezing temperatures. The result: Continental ice sheets and polar ice sheets expanded, and *mountain glaciers* came to town.

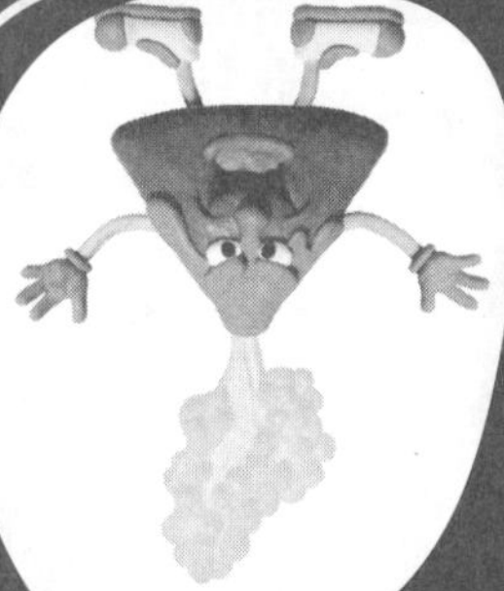

biology

Q: **WHAT** is white light?

earth science

Q: WHEN did the most recent ice age begin and end?

A: *The angle of incidence.* What's that, you ask? First you have to know the *normal.* (That's the imaginary line that's always perpendicular to the surface.) When the surface is exactly horizontal, the normal is exactly vertical. If the angle of reflection comes in at a 50° angle from the surface, the remaining 40° between the reflection and the right angle of the normal is the angle of incidence.

A: The most recent ice age ended about 12,000 years ago. It began about 72,000 years ago. In the United States it's called the Wisconsin glaciation, and in England it's the Devensian glaciation. Either way, it was cold.

biology

Q: WHAT is equal to the angle of reflection in a light beam?

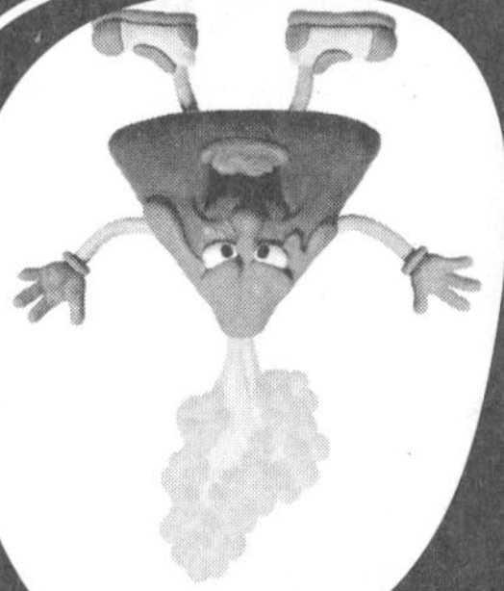

earth science

Q: **WHAT** was the impact of the last ice age on animal life?

A: Light travels in straight lines, as long as it's traveling through a medium that doesn't change.

A: There was a mass extinction of many birds and large mammals, including saber-toothed cats, giant sloths, mammoths, mastodons, and other big beasts known scientifically as Pleistocene megafauna and, informally, as "big scary things."

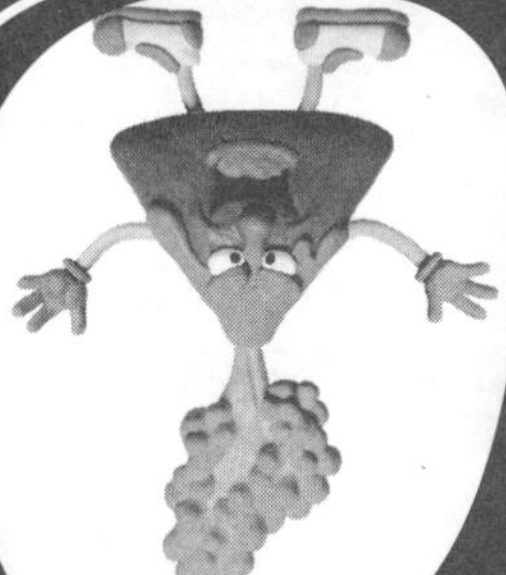

Q: **HOW** does light naturally travel: in straight lines or in changing waves?

biology

earth science

Q: **WHEN** is the next ice age coming?

A: Light. This was not a trick question.

A: Yes, there *will* be a next one. Ice ages generally occur every 40,000 years, though the last few occurred after 100,000-year intervals. So we can safely guess the next big chill will be between 30,000 to 90,000 years from now. For the record, this epoch between ice ages is called MIS-1, or the Flandrian interglacial, if you're British. Either way, it's a lot warmer than an ice age.

biology

Q: WHAT must be present (in addition to your eyes) so you can see something?

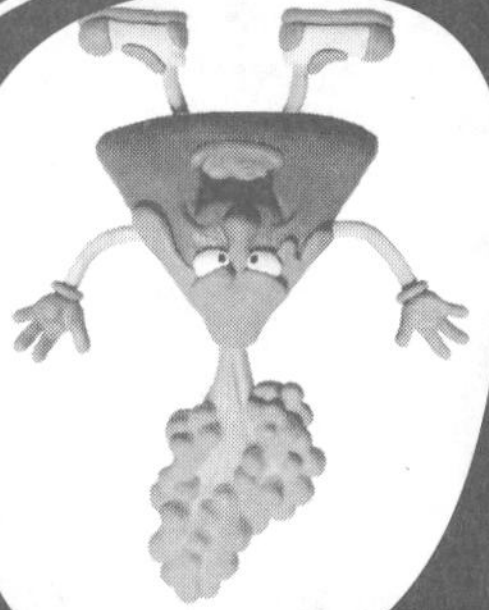

earth science

Q: WHAT geologic epoch and period are we currently in?

A: The atmosphere involves everything in the air.

A: Welcome to the Holocene epoch, which is about 12,000 years old. It's the most current part of the Neogene period, which began about 23 million years ago and is still going strong.

biology

Q: **WHAT** on Earth is the *atmosphere?*

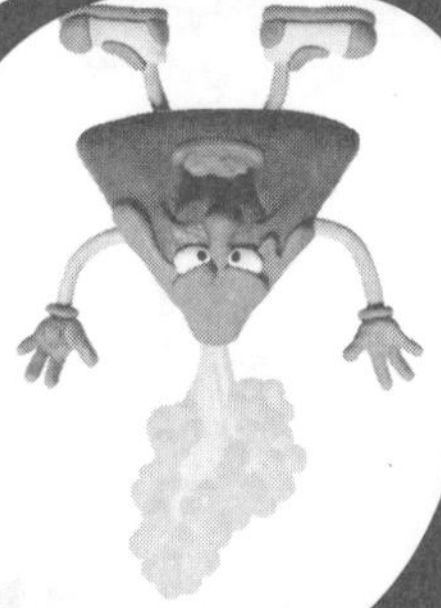

Q: **WHEN** did the first hominids appear on Earth, and why aren't they called *humanoids*?

A: The fresh water we drink comes from wells and other underground sources, as well as from lakes, rivers, glaciers, and plastic bottles.

A: A *hominid* is any member of the "great apes" biological family (*hominidae*). This includes, gorillas, orangutans, chimpanzees, and all you humans. Hominids appeared between 4 and 5 million years ago (though a 2002 discovery may up that to 7 million years ago). Anyone whose body resembles a human is a *humanoid*, including aliens, robots, and our hairy ancestors. But that's much more a term of science fiction than science fact.

biology

Q: **WHICH** major sources provide our planet's drinking water?

earth science

Q: WHEN did the first actual humans appear on Earth?

A: In order of author's preference: snow, rain, hail, and sleet. The author loves snow, and likes the occasional rainstorm, but can really do without sleet. And hail, under the right circumstances, is pretty cool.

A: The first humans (*homo sapiens*) reported for duty between 1.6 and 2 million years ago, depending on which websites you frequent. And, because we never shy away from controversy, we'd like to report that our closest living relative is the chimpanzee.

biology

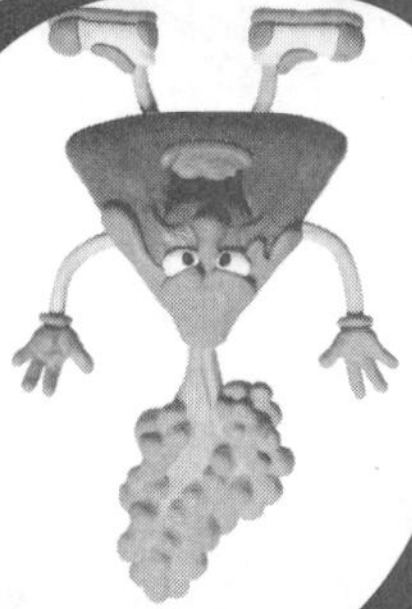

Q: WHAT are the four most common forms of precipitation?

earth science

Q: **WHAT** single factor has the *most* influence on shaping the Earth's landscape?

A: It's called *collection*. And once the water is back in place, it's ready to evaporate all over again.

A: Water—especially water moving downhill. The wash of water across land continues to shape mountains, move rock, dig canyons, create lakes, help rivers grow, irrigate land, distribute soil, and much more.

biology

Q: WHAT is the name of the process by which precipitation refills the rivers, seas, and oceans?

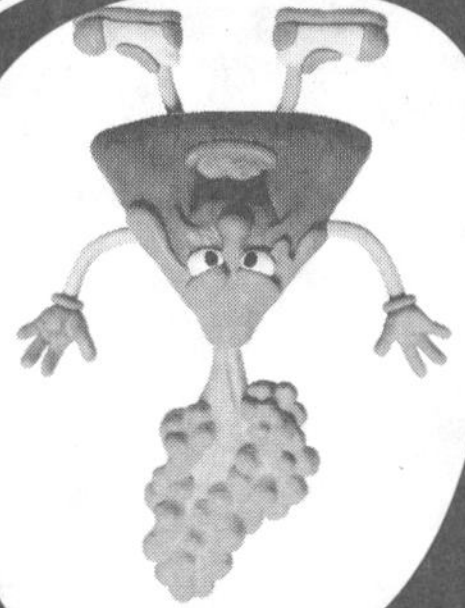

earth science

Q: **WHAT** percentage of the Earth's surface is covered by water?

A: When it rains it pours, and when it pours, it's *precipitation.* Clouds full of condensed air are heavy, so ultimately they return water to the rivers, seas, and oceans.

A: About three-fourths of the Earth (between 70 and 75 percent) is under the wet stuff, including the slowly melting ice caps.

biology

Q: WHAT is the name of the process by which condensed water returns to Earth?

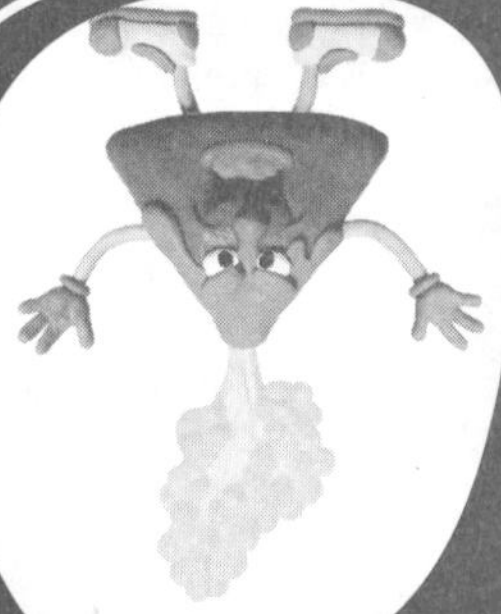

Q: HOW do you rank Earth's oceans, from biggest to smallest?

A: That's *condensation*. As the air gets colder, the vapor forms clouds. And you know what comes next.

A: (1) Pacific, (2) Atlantic, (3) Indian, (4) Antarctic, and (5) Arctic. The Arctic Ocean is the one that surrounds the North Pole. The Antarctic Ocean hugs the South Pole.

biology

Q: **WHAT** is the name of the process by which evaporated water turns back into liquid?

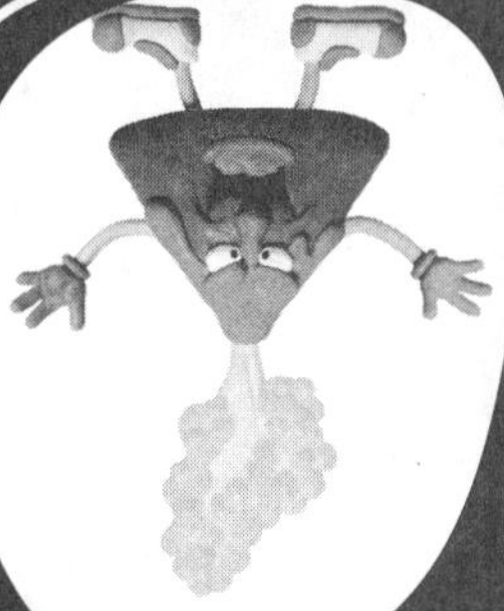

A: It's called *evaporation.* The sun makes the water warmer, warm water becomes steam (or vapor), and up it goes. But don't worry, it'll be back.

earth science

Q: **WHAT** is the average depth of the ocean?

biology

Q: WHAT is the name of the process by which water enters the atmosphere?

A: The average ocean depth is 2.35 *miles* (12,408 feet, or about 10 Empire State Buildings tip to tail).

A: They call it H_2O. H is for hydrogen. O is for oxygen. And salt—the extra ingredient in sea water—is for popcorn.

earth science

Q: **WHERE** is the world's deepest spot?

biology

Q: WHAT are the three main ingredients of sea water?

A: The deepest spot is 6.78 miles (35,800 feet) below sea level. It's the *Marianas Trench*, in the northwest Pacific, not far from Japan.

A: Leaves don't change color—those bright autumn colors *are* the original colors. The green you see in summer comes from chlorophyll, which fades in the cold, dim weather. You could say that leaves change color in the spring, not the fall.

earth science

Q: WHAT are three major topographic features of the ocean?

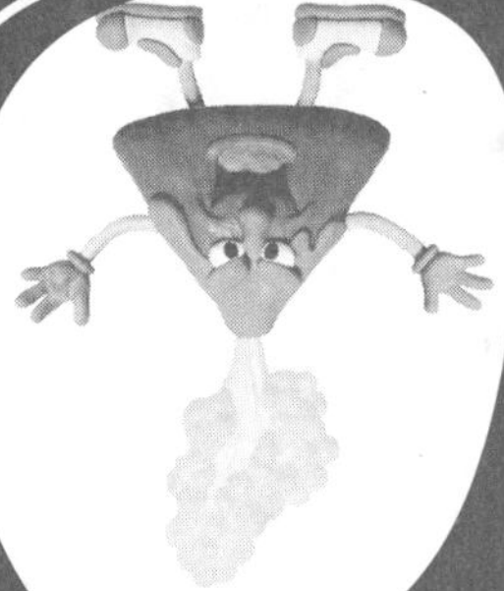

biology

Q: WHY do leaves change color in the fall?

A: Down under, *ocean floors*, *continental margins*, and *mid-ocean ridges* rule. Above ground, Earth's topographic features include mountains, canyons, and flatlands.

A: We call them *chloroplasts.*

Q: **WHAT** do waves carry from place to place?

physics

biology

Q: WHAT do we call a plant's little energy-gathering solar panels that make chlorophyll?

A: Waves carry *energy*, including sound, light, electricity, and hydropower.

A: Chlorophyll. And it's also responsible for giving them their lovely shades of green.

physics

Q: WHAT is *kinetic energy*?

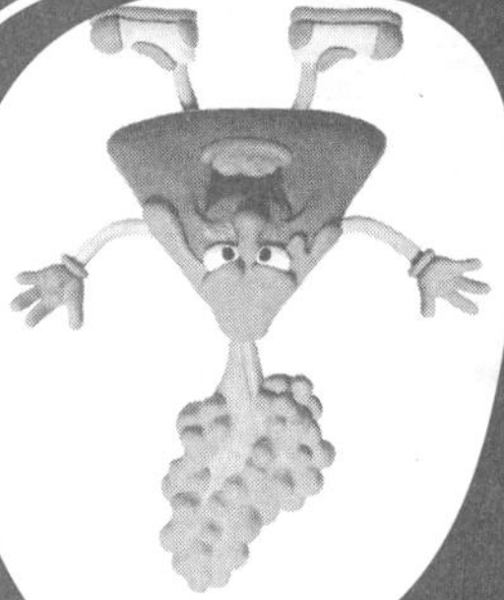

biology

Q: WHAT chemical allows plants to photosynthesize and grow?

A: *Kinetic energy* is the energy created by an object in motion. The energy varies depending on the mass of the object and its velocity. It will keep its kinetic energy until its speed changes.

A: If the plants speak English, they call it *photosynthesis*. In Spanish it's *fotosíntesis*.

physics

Q: **WHAT** do bodies in motion tend to do?

biology

Q: WHAT do plants call their ability to turn sunlight into energy?

A: They tend to stay in motion, until something acts on them (meaning, stops them). This is called *Newton's first law of motion.*

A: It's oxygen.

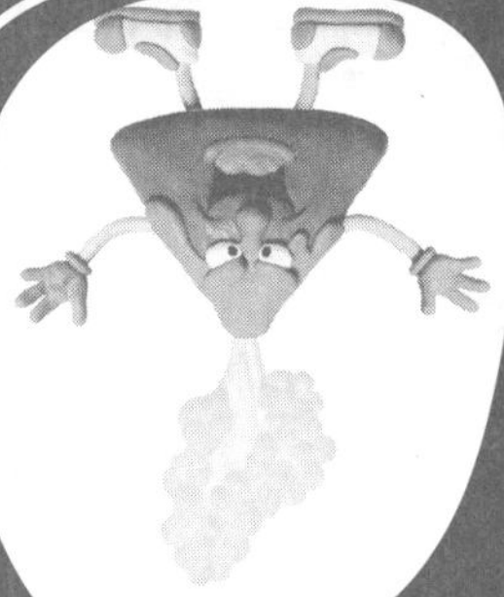

physics

Q: WHAT do bodies at rest tend to do?

biology

Q: WHAT is the waste product that green plants leak into the air?

A: They tend to stay at rest, until something acts on them (meaning, gets them going). This is the second half of *Newton's first law of motion.*

A: The *eardrum*, or *tympanic membrane*. By vibrating, it transmits sound to the middle ear.

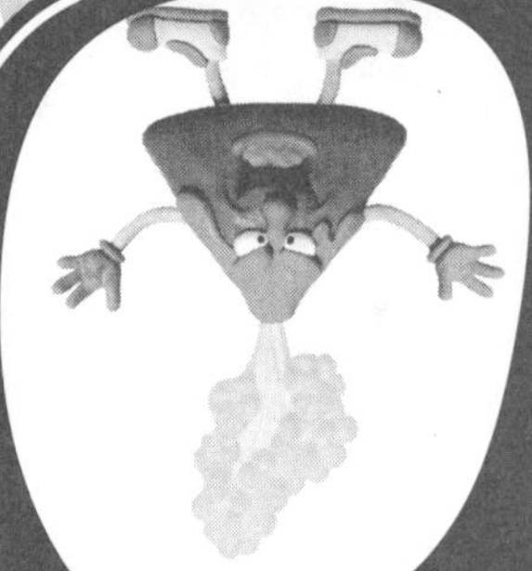

Q: **WHAT** is the result of every action, at least as far as Newton's third law of motion goes?

physics

biology

Q: WHAT is the name of the part of the ear that actually does the hearing?

A: For every action, there is an equal and opposite reaction. A pool cue hitting a billiard ball is a good example of this law in motion.

A: The *pupil*. It dilates (opens larger) in low light, to let more light in, and it contracts (becomes smaller) in bright light, to keep the light from burning little holes into your brain. Kidding.

physics

Q: HOW much energy is needed to return a body in motion back to a state of rest—more, less, or the same amount of energy needed for acceleration?

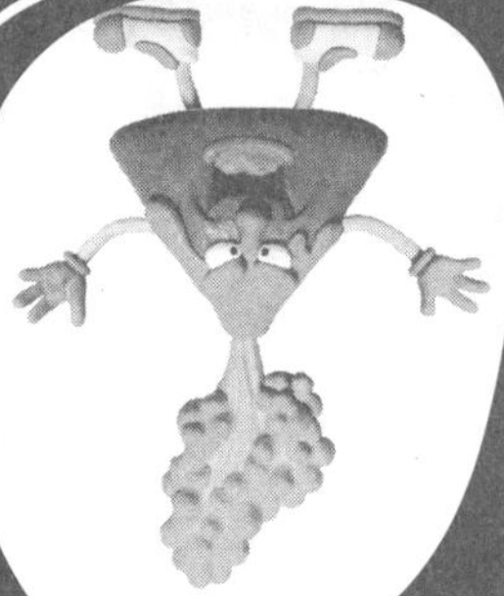

biology

Q: **WHICH** part of the human eye changes size depending on the available light?

A: Twice as much, actually. No matter what speed you are traveling at, you need to use (or lose) twice as much energy to stop.

A: Pollen, ovules, seeds, and fruit.

physics

Q: **WHAT** is the *velocity* of an object?

biology

Q: WHAT are the four parts of a flowering plant's reproductive system?

A: The *velocity* of an object is the rate at which an object changes its position. Jumping up and down in place is motion, but it isn't velocity, because you don't leave your starting position. Only by scooting away from your starting point at top speed will you maximize your velocity.

physics

Q: WHAT two factors must be determined in order to describe the velocity of an object?

A: To provide nutrition to the fetus, and to remove waste.

biology

Q: **WHAT** is the job of the placenta during pregnancy?

A: The *direction* of the object (say, straight down as opposed to straight up), and the *speed* (which, for instance, increases when going straight down, and decreases when going straight up).

A: The male. He provides either the Y chromosome (male) or the X chromosome (female). The female provides only the (female) X chromosome.

physics

Q: WHICH two factors make velocity change?

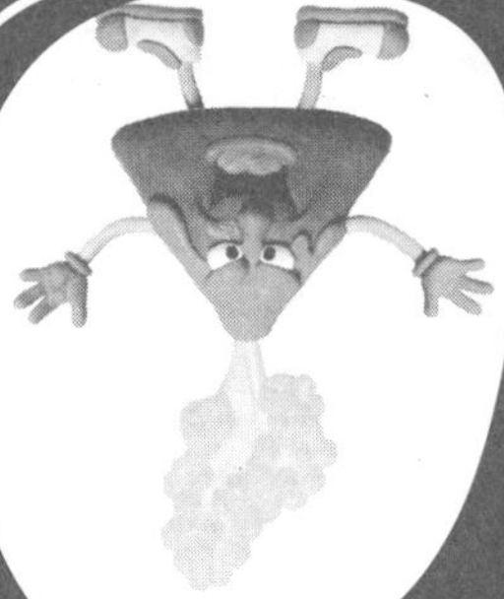

biology

Q: **WHICH** parent determines the gender of its animal offspring?

A: Velocity changes if you make a change in *direction* (a hard right turn) or a change in *speed* (slamming on the brakes), or both (you slam on the brakes before making a hard right turn). In the latter case, your wheels squeal, you kick up some gravel, and your velocity decreases; when the police do the same thing, and your velocity increases again, tell them it's your physics homework that made you do it.

A: Male and female. The male provides the sperm, and the female provides the egg.

physics

Q: HOW do you determine your average speed?

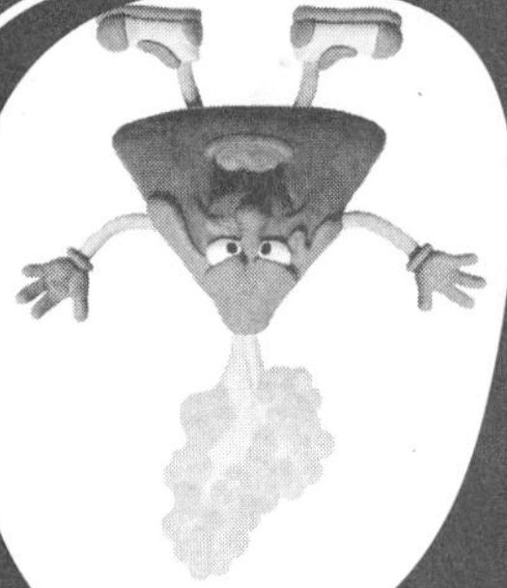

biology

Q: WHICH two genders are necessary for sexual reproduction?

A: Divide the total distance you've traveled by the total time that's elapsed. Remember, your speed may have varied along the way. That's why it's called an average.

A: Your respiratory system (from lips to lungs and beyond) has the endless task of getting oxygen from *out there* and bringing it into your body. Once you've got it, the oxygen is very quickly distributed via your circulatory system to all of your tissues (which are responsible for making those neverending requests for oxygen.)

physics

Q: **WHY** do atoms and molecules move in random patterns in liquids?

biology

Q: WHAT exactly is the main reason you even have a respiratory system?

A: Because the molecular forces between them aren't strong enough to hold the atoms in a solid form.

A: According to your lungs, the stars of your respiratory system are, first, the air intake systems, otherwise known as *your nose* and *mouth*. Next, the underrated *epiglottis* (part of your voice box) decides what goes into your lungs and what goes into your stomach. Without it, you actually *would* inhale your food. And finally the *trachea*, or windpipe, channels all that fresh air straight to your lungs.

physics

Q: **WHAT**, in physics, is *force*?

biology

Q: **WHICH** four body parts take the leading roles bringing air to your lungs?

A: A *force* is an action, impact, or other cause that's responsible for a change in the recipient's "system." (Think of bat against baseball, or yo-yo against string.) Any action requiring energy involves some amount of force.

A: Bones and muscles are what move you.

physics

Q: WHAT are the two kinds of forces?

biology

Q: WHAT two parts of an animal's structural framework are necessary for movement?

A: There are *contact* forces and *field* forces. When one object has physical contact with another (finger against doorbell or air into balloon), that's contact force. On the other hand, magnets and gravity are field forces. No contact is necessary.

A: All of them: Failure of the organs, tissues, or cells can be fatal. Or, on a better day, failure could just give you a bad stomachache.

Q: WHAT two characteristics are always present in force?

physics

biology

Q: WHICH part of an organ system can be fatal if it fails?

A: For a force to be a force, it needs to have *direction* (so that it can get to the thing it's going to affect) and *magnitude* (the ability to actually make an impact on something else).

A: Individual organs, tissues, and cells. (If you said keyboard, pipes, and a stool, you'd also be right, but for different reasons.)

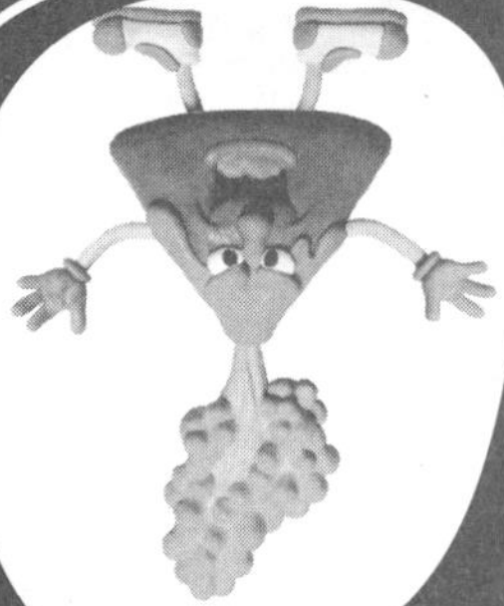

physics

Q: **WHAT** happens when an object is affected by two or more forces at once?

biology

Q: **WHAT** are the three parts of an organ system?

A: When more than one force is with you, the result is a cumulative effect of all of the forces. Imagine you're under a rock avalanche. Then you can see how forces can really add up.

A: Mechanical, chemical, and physical functions.

physics

Q: WHAT happens when the forces on an object are balanced?

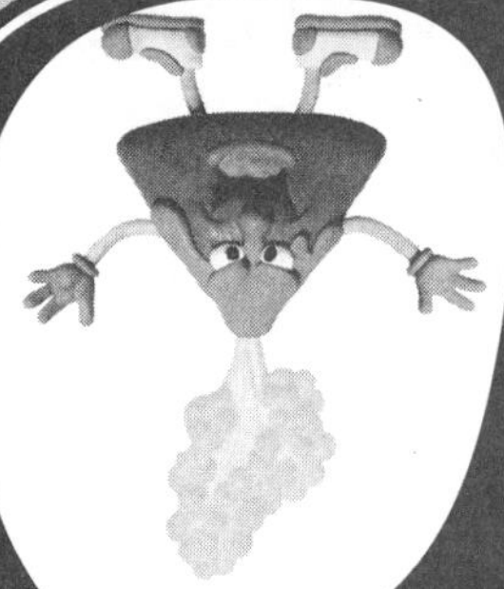

biology

Q: WHAT are the three kinds of functions in an organism?

A: When the forces are balanced the motion of the object remains unchanged, whether or not it was moving at the time of impact.

A: It's the study of the structure and function of the organism.

physics

Q: WHAT happens when the forces on an object are unbalanced?

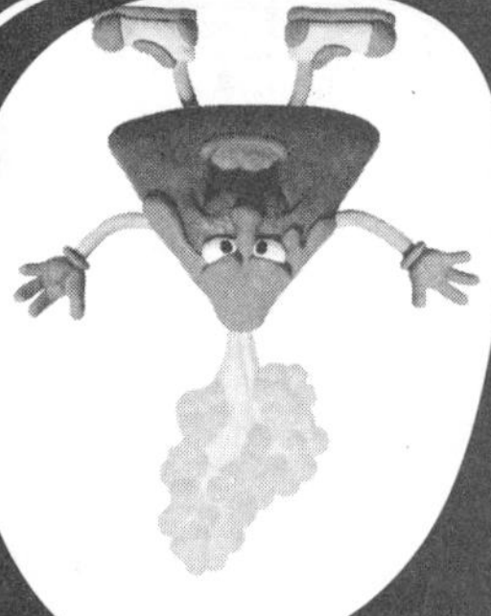

biology

Q: WHAT do we mean when we describe an organism's *physiology*?

A: The velocity of the object will change—faster or slower, and changes direction, too. May they be with you.

A: Ice ages and human meddling change climates slowly. However, the Earth speeds things up the old-fashioned way: with volcanoes, floods, earthquakes, and landslides. The faster, the scarier.

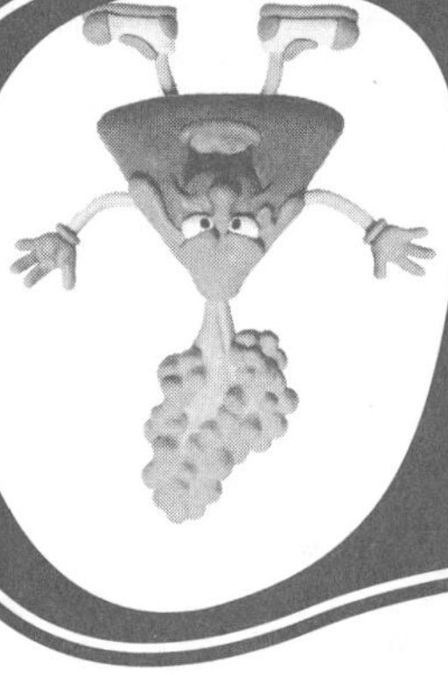

physics

Q: **WHEN** the mass of an object increases, does it require more or less force to remain in motion at the same speed?

biology

Q: HOW can the Earth change a habitat immediately?

A: More. More. More. More. Picture six more clowns piled into a little car already filled with clowns—the car's engine would require a lot more force to get them to the circus on time.

A: Rivers are dynamic, active systems. They expand, they erode, they move in new directions, they carry sediment, and they sometimes share more water than their neighbors would like.

physics

Q: WHAT is equilibrium?

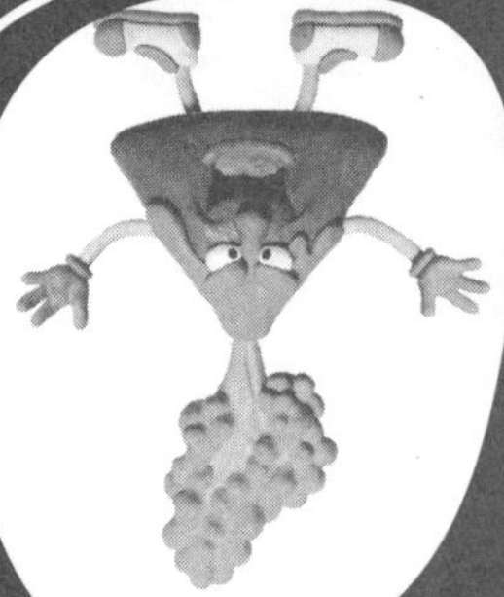

biology

Q: WHICH kind of system is a river: static or dynamic?

A: Any object (say, a bust of Beethoven) is always subject to forces. When the object is at rest, all the forces that act on the object (the gravity, and the force the table exerts to hold Beethoven up) cancel each other out. Therefore, the combination of all the forces (the *net force*) equals zero. With a net force of zero, you've got *equilibrium.*

A: The *hydrosphere* is every part of the planet that's filled with water.

physics

Q: HOW would you describe an object moving at constant, unchanged velocity: Is it in equilibrium or not?

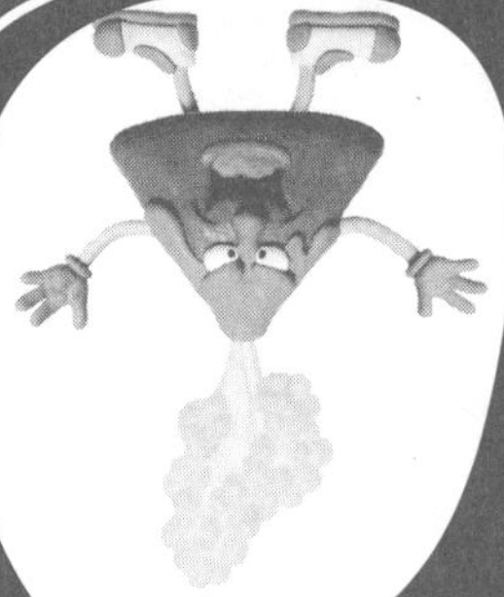

biology

Q: **WHAT** on Earth is the *hydrosphere*?

A: Any object moving at constant velocity (think of a meteor) is not accelerating or slowing down, so its net force is zero, just as if it weren't moving. Therefore, that object is in equilibrium. *Now you know why rolling stones need not gather moss.*

A: The *biosphere* is every part of the planet where life occurs.

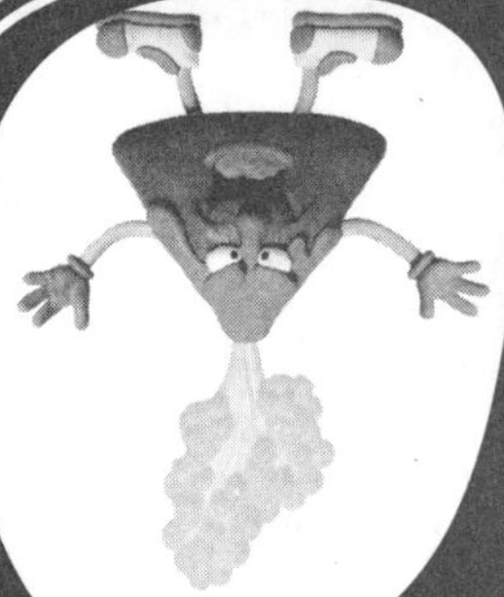

Q: WHAT is *gravity?*

physics

biology

Q: WHAT on Earth is the *biosphere*?

A: *Gravity* is a force. It's the attraction between any two objects, regardless of mass, size, or form. And, when one of the objects is a planet, it pretty much sets the rules for anything smaller.

A: Skin is a shield, giving you lots of defenses against infection. Skin also keeps your insides in and the outside out.

physics

Q: WHAT is the difference between weight and mass?

biology

Q: WHICH health benefits does your skin provide?

A: The mass of something is defined by the quantity of molecules, electrons, protons, neutrons, and so on. Weight is relative to the attraction force of something huge, like a planet. That's why we have different weights on different planets, but our mass remains the same (except for the additional space suit).

A: The environment changes (perhaps because of a glacier, or a lack of food, or a hungry new predator), and the species can't adequately adapt. This is infrequently known as the un-survival of the un-fittest.

Q: WHY is the Moon's gravity less than Earth's?

physics

biology

Q: WHAT is the usual cause for a species' extinction?

A: It's not really because the Moon is smaller than the Earth. It has more to do with Earth having more mass, and therefore a greater gravitational effect. The gravity on the Moon is about one-sixth of Earth's, which means you 200-pounders would weigh 34 pounds. That's quite a jump.

physics

Q: WHAT does a 100-pound person weigh on Jupiter?

A: Adapt, leave, or die.

biology

Q: WHICH three choices are available to an organism whose environment has just changed?

A: Jupiter's gravity is 2.54 times greater than Earth's gravity. So, a 100-pounder would weigh 254 pounds, and move slowly, too. Interestingly (for some), Jupiter's mass is actually 317 times the mass of Earth, but due to some complicated math, you wouldn't weigh 31,700 pounds if you visited. You'd never leave.

A: They help scientists group and classify organisms by species, genus, and so on up the ladder.

physics

Q: **WHAT** are some of the key effects of gravity here on Earth?

biology

Q: HOW are shared, derived, and observable characteristics of living organisms handy to scientists?

A: Gravity keeps the Earth's atmosphere, oceans, and inhabitants from drifting into space. Gravity pulls the rain to the rivers, and ultimately to the sea. Gravity guides the development and growth of plants and affects the way our bones and muscles develop and function. And gravity keeps us from floating out of convertible cars.

A: All of the above.

physics

Q: **WHAT** is the effect of gravity on the solar system?

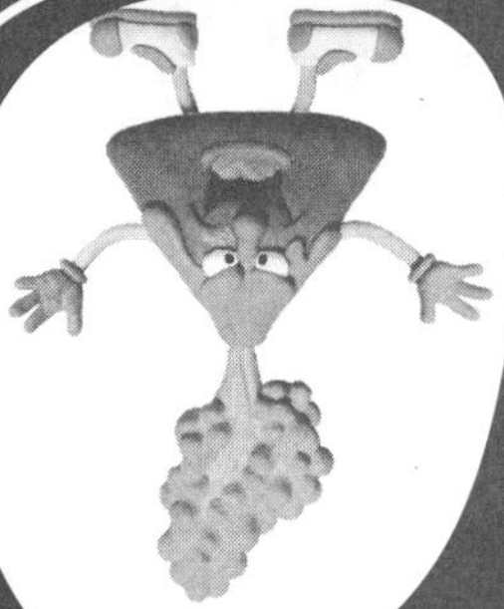

biology

Q: WHICH of these categories form the basis of evolutionary science: (1) comparative anatomy, (2) fossils, or (3) geology?

A: Gravity holds the Earth and its eight (or so) planetary friends in their orbit around the Sun. It's a real testimony to the influence (and mass) of the Sun that it can keep its grip on not only Earth, but Pluto, over a billion miles away.

physics

Q: WHY is Earth, and basically everything else in space, a sphere?

A: Darwin called that *natural selection.*

biology

Q: WHAT is the official term for "survival of the fittest"?

A: Because gravity pulls in all directions with equal force. So, each surface on an object (a rock, a planet, etc.) ultimately will end up the same distance from the object's core. Any variations (from collisions or breakaways) will gradually be forced by the object's gravitational forces back into the shape of a sphere.

A: *Mutation.* If a much larger offspring appears, say, and begins to pass that trait along to its descendants, then height will have evolved in that species.

physics

Q: WHICH direction does heat flow between cold things and hot things?

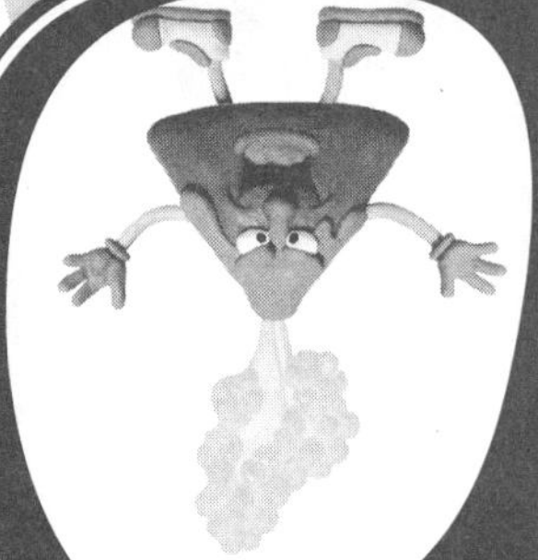

biology

Q: **WHAT** *can cause a species to evolve quickly?*

A: Heat flows *from* the hot thing *to* the cold thing until they're equally warm things.

A: A naturalist named Charles Darwin. In 1831, he went sailing to the isolated Galapagos Islands, saw the diversity that nature is capable of, and got to thinking.

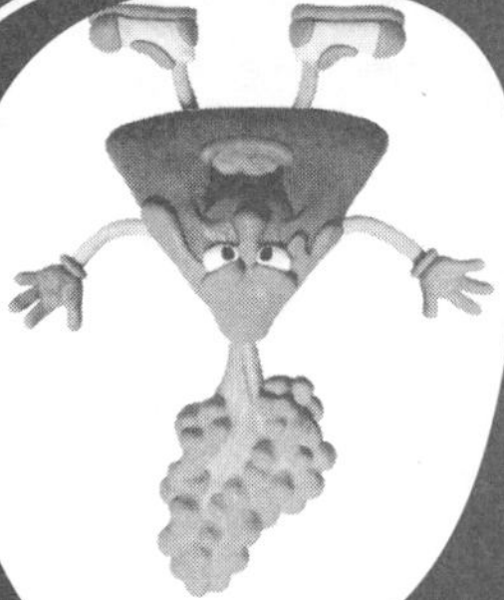

physics

Q: WHAT happens to the energy that's released when fuel is consumed?

Q: **WHO** is the scientist who discovered evolution?

A: The energy becomes *heat energy*. That's why the burning logs, the car engine, and your average flamethrower are hot.

A: Genetic variation will make the difference, and environmental factors will, too.

physics

Q: **HOW** does heat flow through solid objects?

biology

Q: WHICH two key factors prompt evolution and diversity of species?

A: Heat is *conducted* through solid objects—transmitted across matter, without matter actually flowing through those objects. Think of a metal pot conducting the heat of the stove it's on.

A: Evolution, my dear Watson!

physics

Q: HOW does heat flow through liquid objects?

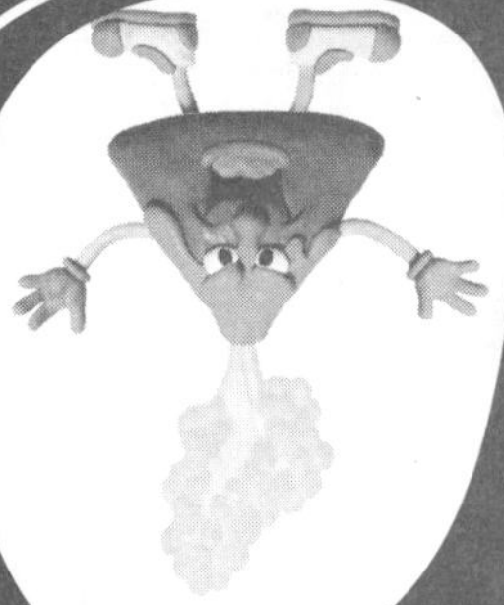

biology

Q: WHAT is the term for gradual change among a species?

A: Two ways. By *conduction*—think of a pot of water boiling on a stove (see previous question). Heat also flows by *convection*, because of matter flowing. Think of that boiling water being poured into cold water, and the heat spreading.

A: Dominant genes get passed along, while recessive genes don't. And then suddenly, after eleven generations or so, two recessive genes team up, and a blue-eyed kid shows up in a brown-eyed family.

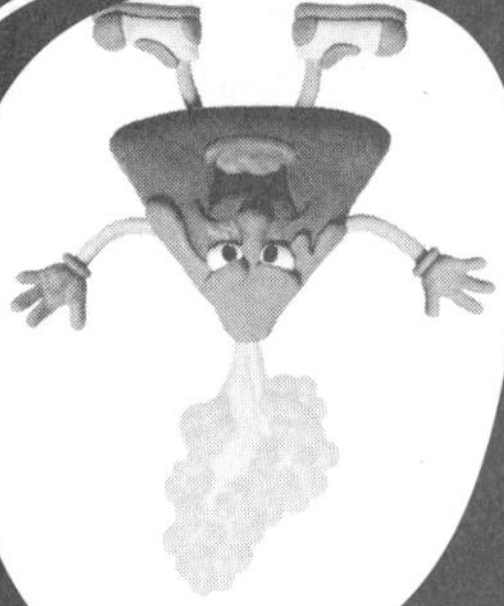

Q: HOW does heat flow through space?

physics

biology

Q: WHICH genes in an allele get their traits passed along, and which don't?

A: *By radiation.* It can radiate from the Sun, 93 million miles away, or from a lightbulb on your desk. Don't touch!

physics

Q: HOW does the heat in the Earth's mantle get to the surface: by conduction or convection?

A: Alleles (Uh-LEELS).

biology

Q: WHAT are the set of copies of genes called?

A: By *convection*. It flows upward mostly via red-hot magma that flows as it reaches the surface. Magma either boils the water or bubbles up as lava.

A: Two copies. One from each parent. Incidentally, they may not be identical.

physics

Q: WHAT carries energy from place to place?

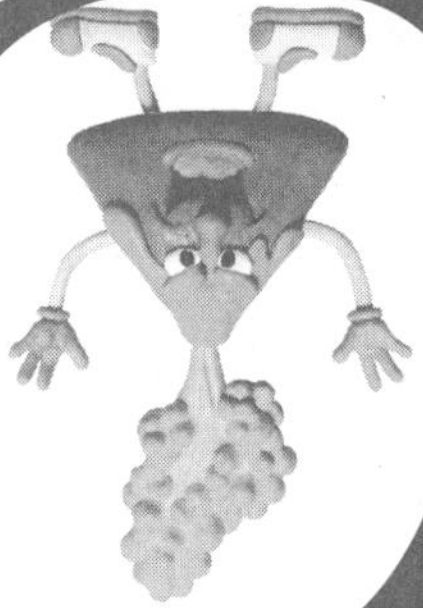

biology

Q: **HOW** many copies of each gene do plants, animals, and middle-school students have?

A: Anything that moves can carry energy. That includes raindrops, rolling stones, any kind of waves (sound waves, light waves, ocean waves), burning fuel, heat flow, wind, and everything else that doesn't stand still.

A: In the *chromosomes*. They're big molecules (macromolecules, actually) that have the job of holding all the genetic information together.

physics

Q: WHAT form does solar energy take as it reaches Earth?

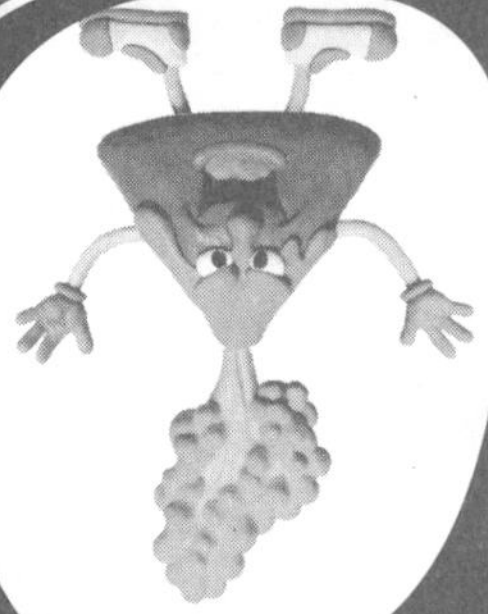

biology

Q: WHERE does DNA live in a cell?

A: Solar energy is radiation that arrives mainly as *light*. Visible light. The light is bright and the light is hot, but first and foremost, it's light.

A: It's DNA, to be precise. Its full name is deoxyribonucleic acid, so if you were being *really* precise, its initials would be DORNA.

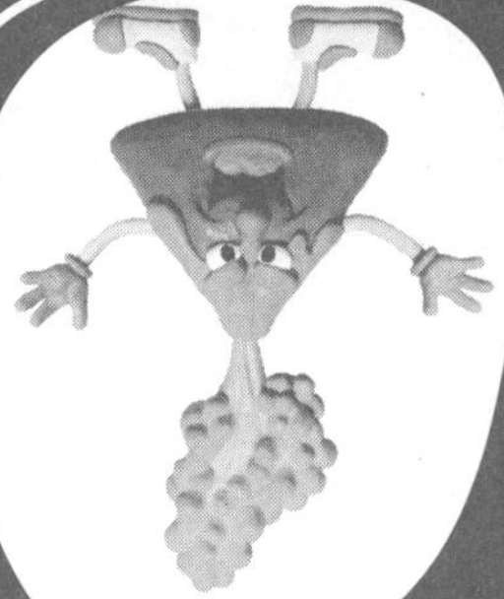

physics

Q: WHAT is a *joule?*

biology

Q: WHAT is the three-letter name of the organic material that carries genetic information in all living organisms?

A: A *joule* is the standard unit of heat energy. According to legend (and several websites), a joule is the energy required to lift a small, 3.5 oz. apple 3 feet in the air against Earth's gravity.

A: Either. Simple traits, like earlobe shape and dimples, come from one gene. Complex traits, like behavior, come from multiple genes.

physics

Q: **WHAT** is the difference between an insulator, an insulter, and an incubator?

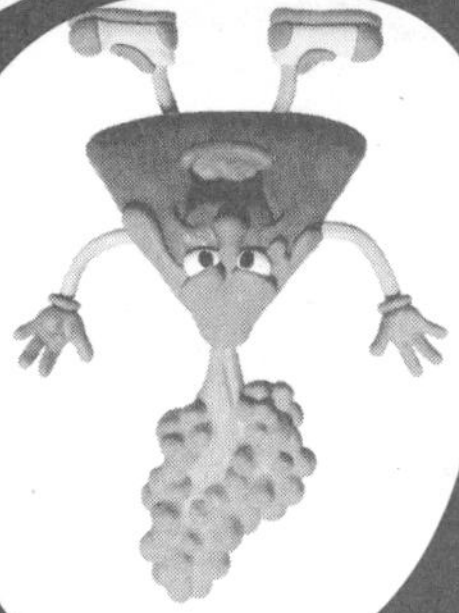

biology

Q: **HOW** many genes does it take to determine an inherited trait: one or more?

A: *Insulators* are substances that don't easily conduct heat or electricity. *Insulters* don't conduct themselves nicely in public. *Incubators* conduct eggs into chicks using heat and light.

physics

Q: WHAT is the difference between *nuclear fusion* and *nuclear fission*?

A: They get half from each parent.

biology

Q: HOW do sexually reproduced organisms get their genes?

A: With *fusion*, a larger nucleus is created from smaller ones. (The sun is a nuclear fusion furnace, turning hydrogen into helium and releasing a great amount of energy in the process.) With *fission*, an atom's nucleus is split apart. (This creates massive amounts of energy that can power a city, or even a submarine.)

A: Environmental influences. For instance, if you grow up in a jungle and your identical twin grows up in Antarctica, you will each look quite different at your fiftieth birthday reunion.

physics

Q: **WHAT** makes the wind blow: gravity, the Sun, or the Moon?

biology

Q: WHAT can affect traits beside the genetic instructions?

A: The *Sun* is the one. Heated air rises, and cooler air falls in the process called *convection*. This ongoing up-and-down activity causes the back-and-forth action we call *wind*.

A: They specify the traits of the cell. Traits are everything you inherited from Mom and Dad, especially how you look. From hair color to toe length, you can't trade your traits.

physics

Q: WHICH type of current makes the air and the oceans warm?

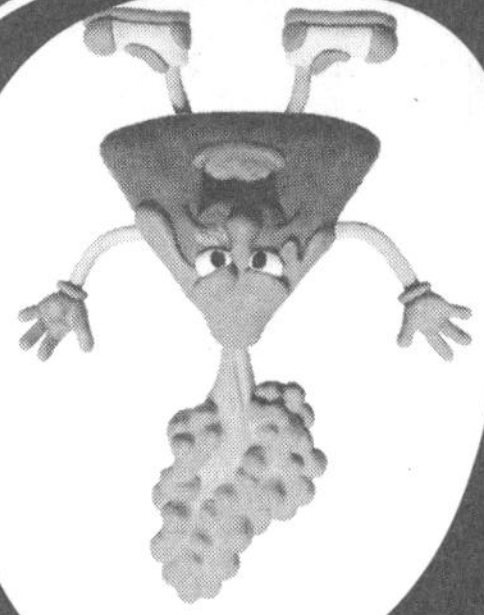

biology

Q: WHAT is the importance of a cell's genetic instructions?

A: *Convection currents.* While the warmer air rises and cooler air falls, the wind they create spreads warm air throughout the geosphere.

A: In the nucleus, remember? We told you that a few questions ago.

physics

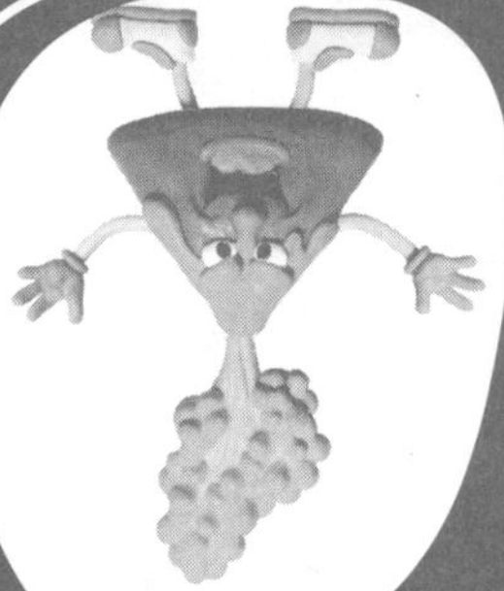

Q: **WHICH** four factors take the most blame for changing the weather?

biology

Q: WHERE is genetic information in a cell found?

A: Heat, humidity, air pressure, and air currents—and not always in that order, depending on where you're talking about.

A: A *cytoskeleton* helps the cell keep its shape, and its contents, in order. Think of a gooey plastic bag. To a cell, that's a skeleton.

physics

Q: **WHAT** is *air pressure?*

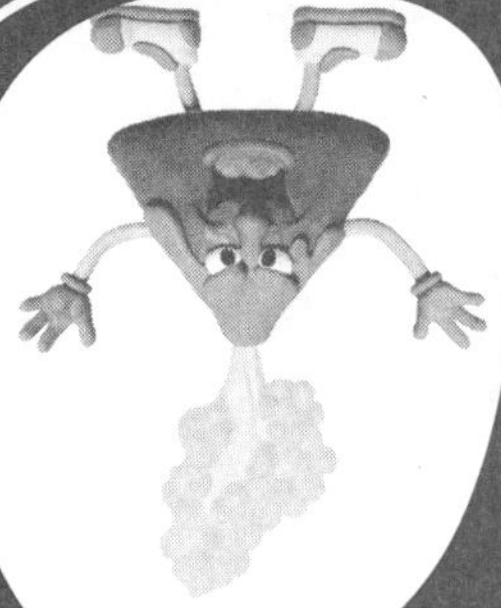

biology

Q: WHAT is a cytoskeleton?

A: *Air pressure* (or *atmospheric pressure*) is literally the pressure that the weight of air causes in the Earth's atmosphere. The atmosphere is actually pressing against you at over 14 pounds of pressure per square inch. Feel the squeeze? When it's most compressed, the weatherman calls it a *high pressure* system. To see what *you* call it, see the next question.

A: Because back in 1665, British scientist Robert Hooke stared at a cork through an ancient microscope, saw the honeycomb of cells, and thought they looked like the small dormitory cells where monks slept in monasteries.

physics

Q: **WHICH** do you prefer: a *high pressure* system or a *low pressure* system?

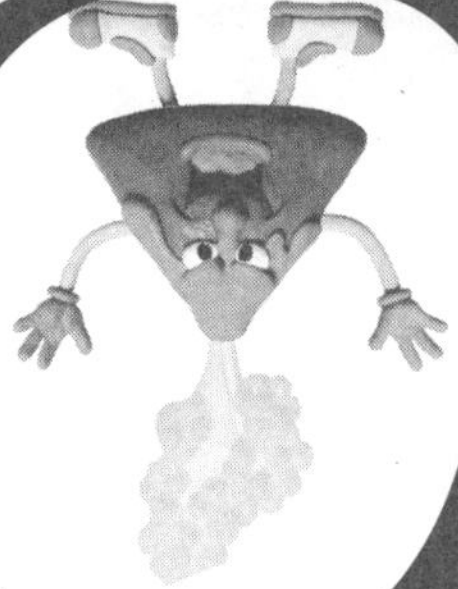

biology

Q: WHY are cells called "cells"?

A: There's no correct answer. With a *high pressure* system, temperatures usually cool down, and skies clear up. With a *low pressure* system, you can expect warmer weather but also storms and rain. We prefer cooler and sunnier, in case you're interested.

A: They *differentiate*, which means they go through the normal process of maturing, which means they can do the jobs they're supposed to do.

physics

Q: **WHAT** are the three most common means of transferring energy?

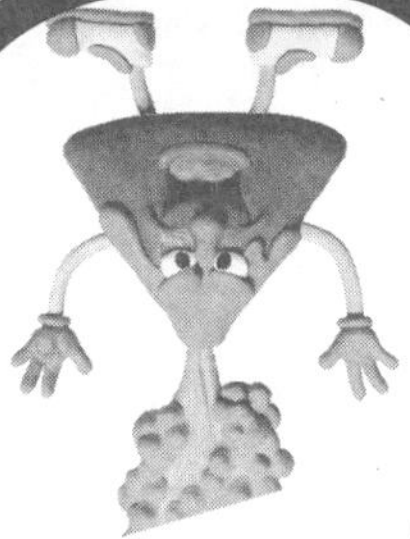

biology

Q: WHEN multicellular organisms develop, what happens to all their multicells?

A: Convection, conduction, and radiation.

A: Yes—mitosis is not only ongoing, it's the basis of the continuance of life. Remember, all cells exist because of cell division.

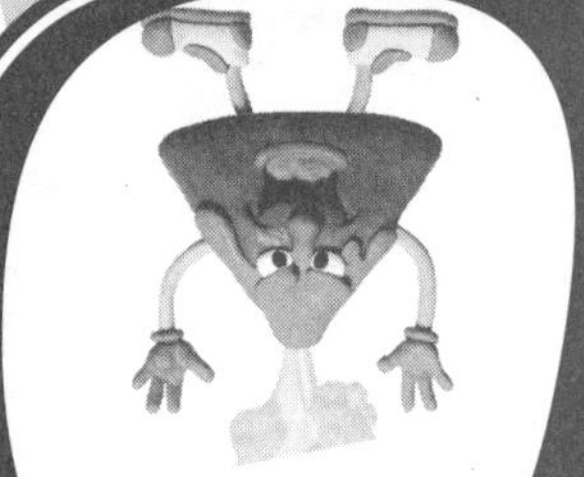

Q: **HOW** is heat transferred by convection?

physics

biology

Q: WHEN daughter cells grow up to become parent cells, can they divide again?

A: Heat is transferred by convection when it comes in waves. The waves can be electric waves, or within a fluid, or the result of force.

A: They're the twin result of mitosis—identical cells with identical sets of chromosomes that come from the parent cell. You could say that mitosis is splitting up for the sake of the kids.

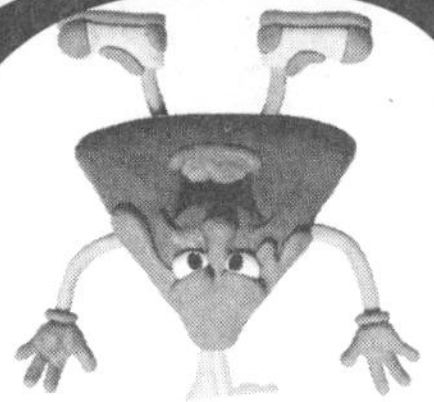

Q: WHERE is heat usually transferred by convection?

physics

biology

Q: **WHO** are the daughter cells?

A: Convection heat gets around everywhere: It regularly occurs in the Earth's mantle, in the oceans, and in the atmosphere.

A: Through mitosis, when they divide.

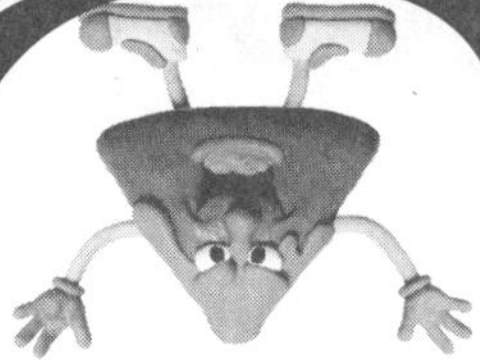

Q: HOW is heat transferred by conduction?

physics

biology

Q: HOW do cells increase their population?

A: Something gets hot (say, something metal) and then it stays hot for a while, and then something touches it (say, your hand) and *that* gets hot, too. *Voila!* The metal thing has conducted the heat. And now you're reversing the effect under cold water.

A: From a parent cell splitting in half. Yes, sir, that's *mitosis*. And it is understood that all cells on Earth come from a single source. Therefore, way, way back, there was *just* one cell. Where it came from is the source of all kinds of debates.

physics

Q: **HOW** is heat transferred by radiation?

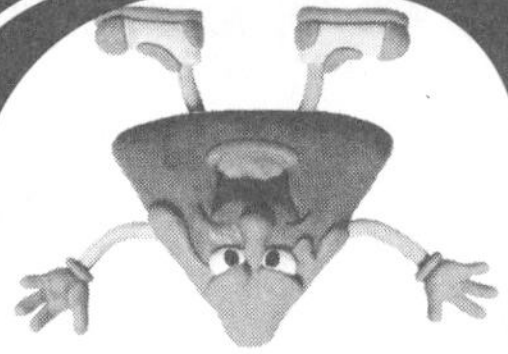

Q: **WHERE** do cells come from?

A: Radiation, or *radiant heat*, is heat that comes directly from something that's hot, like the Sun (or a *radiator*). The hotter the hot thing is, the hotter the air around it will be. The farther you are from the hot thing, the cooler it gets. Make sense?

A: The "Big M" are organelles that turn nutrients into energy for the cells. The *mitochondria* are the principal energy source of the cell.

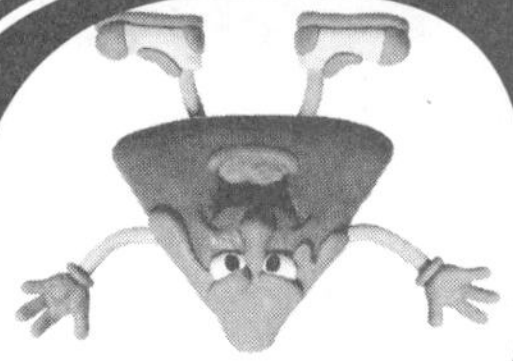

physics

Q: **WHAT** is the definition of *density*?

biology

Q: WHAT *do mitochondria do?*

A: *Density* is the mass within a unit volume. (The units can be cubic inches or square miles.) The more mass, the more dense.

A: *Organelles* are way smaller than animal organs, but they work the same way. For instance, each organelle in a cell has a different function, and a different shape, and a different name. See what we mean?

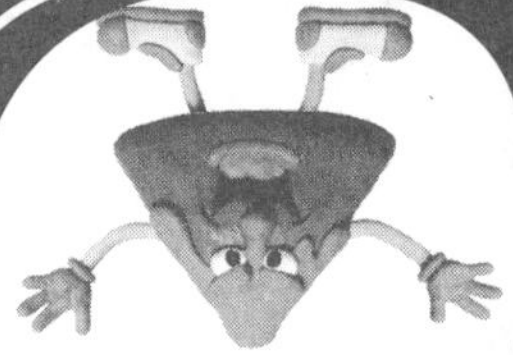

Q: WHAT is the difference between regular solids and irregular ones?

physics

biology

Q: WHAT *are organelles?*

A: Spheres and cubes are regular solids, and it's easy to measure their density and volume. Snakes, trees, philosophers, and royal crowns are irregular solids. It takes a lot more math to calculate those measurements. Incidentally a *hebesphenomegacorona* is an irregular solid figure with 21 faces (18 triangular, the other 3 square), looking like a golf ball shaved by a hatchet.

A: The *nucleus* is the part of the cell that is responsible for growth, storing genetic information, and reproduction. If you're looking for a reproduction joke here, forget it.

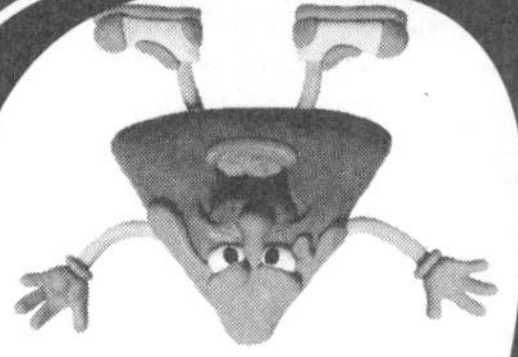

Q: **WHY** do air bubbles rise?

physics

biology

Q: WHAT is the *nucleus* of a cell?

A: As you learned in your first bathtub, bubbles rise to the surface. The air in those bubbles is displacing (or shoving aside) the water it's next to. But the water doesn't *want* to be shoved aside. *So* it shoves back with equal force, and squeezes the bubbles to the top. The measurable force of that water shoving back is called *buoyant force*.

A: It's a *semipermeable membrane.* It regulates the ways a cell interacts with its environment, and it keeps the cell's tiny parts from wandering. (FYI, the name "Semipermeable Membrane" is still available for your garage rock band.)

physics

Q: HOW do you determine the buoyant force of an object?

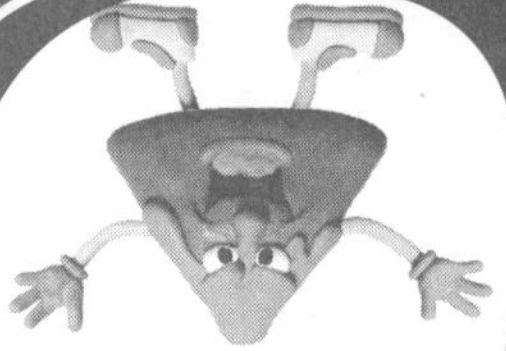

biology

Q: WHAT is the outside "skin" of an animal cell called?

A: The buoyant force of an object depends on how dense the liquid is, and how much liquid is being displaced. If the object's weight is less than the weight of the liquid it would displace, then the object is less dense and it will float.

A: We animals have *cell membranes* instead of cell walls, but they do the same job. The plasma membrane separates and protects a cell from its surrounding environment. If you're interested (and if you're not), they're largely made from lipids.

biology

Q: **WHAT** are the "building blocks of life" in all living organisms actually called?

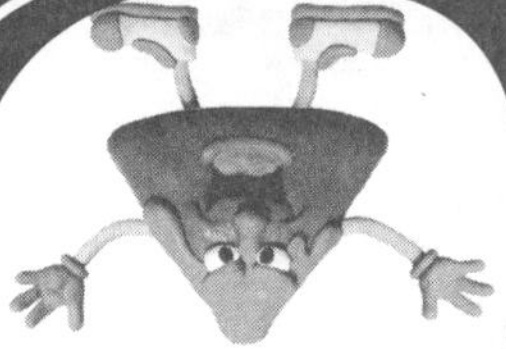

biology

Q: **WHAT** is a *cell membrane?*

A: They're called *cells*. However, being in a "cell block for life" is a whole different matter.

A: Plant cells have a cell wall, chloroplasts, and larger vacuoles. Plant cells also are more rectangular, because their cell walls are more rigid.

biology

Q: HOW few cells can you have and still respectably call yourself an organism?

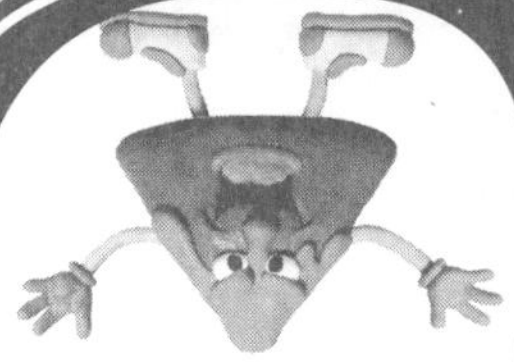

biology

Q: WHAT do plant cells have that animal cells don't?

A: One is enough. The amoeba and bacteria are single-celled, but they're definitely players.

A: A *cell wall* is a flexible, solid layer surrounding the cells of life forms like plants, bacteria, and algae. Usually it takes an enzyme to tear down the wall.

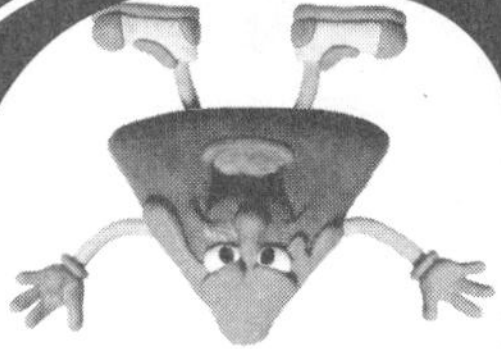

biology

Q: HOW many cells are in the average human?

biology

Q: **WHAT** is a *cell wall*?

A: 100 trillion. Or 10^{14}. Or a lot.

A: Quite similarly. It is the basis of evolutionary science that the cells in all life forms have significant biological similarities due to their common ancestry.

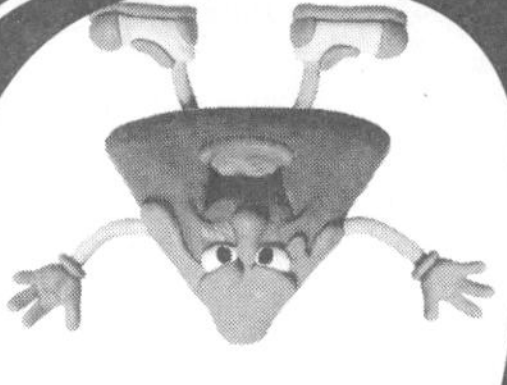

biology

Q: WHAT is directly in front of you if you are looking at a red blood cell?

biology

Q: HOW do cells in different living organisms function—similarly or differently?

A: A microscope. A red blood cell is about 20 micrometers across, or about one-tenth the width of a human hair.

No page numbers!

How do we do it? More importantly, why do we do it? Because each page would have two numbers on it facing in opposite directions, that's why. Isn't an upside-down book covered with little pictures that move strange enough?

Little pictures that move!

Try it for yourself. Hold the book in one hand, and riff the pages with the other. The effect of animation will inspire awe. Perhaps you'll embark on your own career in cartooning—or even writing books like this—all thanks to this *Flip-O-Matic* book.

Happy Flipping!

Welcome back to *Flip-O-Matic!*

We know you're still marveling at the patented *Flip-O-Matic* technology that got you here. Don't panic! It's easy to adjust to reading upside-down.

Now that you're through with the first half of the book, you've probably got a pretty good idea what to expect in the second half of the book. We do, too. Here are some highlights:

More questions!

Your *Flip-O-Matic* book has been packed with twice the information you'd expect in a book this length—twice the information, yet only half the seriousness. How is that possible? Nobody knows!

More answers!

One-hundred percent of the questions in your *Flip-O-Matic* book come complete with answers—and not just any answers! They're appropriate answers based on facts. Without facts, this book would be fiction and fiction books aren't nearly so useful when you're trying to learn science!